The

Rally Course Book

A Guide to AKC Rally Courses

Janice Dearth

Alpine
PUBLICATIONS
Loveland, Colorado

ISBN 1-57779-067-7

Course designs: Janice Dearth
Layout and illustrations: Lisa Dryer
Cover design: Laura Newport

First printing September 2004

3 4 5 6 7 8 9 0

Printed in the United States of America.

Table of Contents

Introduction

This Rally Course book has been created in hopes that exhibitors, instructors, and judges will find it to be an education in teaching, designing, and judging Rally. Section One is aimed toward instructors. Section Two is about designing Rally courses and includes useable AKC Rally courses with Exhibitor sheets. Hopefully this book will stimulate your creative course-designing juices to go beyond the courses I've included. It should also help current judges save some time in designing courses.

The Rally signs in this book are the currently (2004) accepted AKC Non-Regular Obedience Class signs. These are still subject to modifications, as Rally continues moving forward to becoming a titling class. I don't foresee many future sign changes, just a few, if any. If this does take place, you will be able to substitute any changed signs in the prewritten courses included in this book with very little effort. Don't forget to also change the course picture and listed exercises on the exhibitor sheets at the same time.

I've had a good time designing this book! I believe it comes at a crucial time for Rally, as the AKC has now announced that Rally will be a titling class/event beginning January 1, 2005.

At this writing I have judged over 800 handler/dog teams in AKC Rally venues over the last four years. I have used all the courses included in this book at one time or another. Feel free to copy these courses to use for your classes, judging, or seminars. Once you get the hang of it, you'll have fun designing your own courses!

Janice Dearth
August 2004

AKC Non-Regular Obedience Class Judge, #19012
AKC Rally Provisional Judge, all Classes
ASCA Obedience Judge, all Classes
NADOI Endorsed Member, #737 N/O
NADOI List Administrator, NADOI Board of Directors
Pikes Peak Obedience Club, Inc., Colorado Springs, CO, Life Member

Section 1

Instructor and Exhibitor Rally Familiarization

Instructor's Class Syllabus

The beginning Rally student must have some training prerequisites: The dog must be able to walk on a loose lead on the handler's left, have some dog-to-human attention, know how to sit at heel and sit at front, and know how to perform the right and left finish exercises without the handler moving his/her feet. Training of these exercises is NOT covered in this book.

Suggested Class Syllabus (6 weeks, 1-hour class each week)

The instructor should have numbers and signs ready before the start of each class.

Week 1
1. Explanation of Rally, with lots of excitement—5 minutes
2. Instructor/dog demo of heeling with "talking" to the dog—5 minutes
3. Heeling warm-ups with Sits at Heel, emphasize "talking to the dog"—10 minutes
4. Teach Right Turns, work with students individually—10 minutes
5. Set up Right Turn Rally Course #101-1R—5 minutes
6. Walk course with students (preferably without dogs)—5 minutes
7. Students work course—20 minutes

Week 2
1. Dogs and handlers do Heeling warm-up with pattern to include Right Turns—10 minutes
2. Walk through without dogs and run Course #101-2R (includes change of pace and 1-step halt sign)—35 minutes
3. Begin teaching Left Turn signs—15 minutes

Week 3
1. Dogs and handlers do Heeling warm-up with pattern to include Left Turns—10 minutes
2. Walk through without dogs and run Course #102-1L—30 minutes
3. Teach Serpentine, Figure 8, and Spirals (left and right)—10 minutes
4. Teach Come Front, Finish Forward, Finish with Halt signs, both directions—10 minutes

Week 4
1. Dogs and handlers do Heeling warm-up with pattern to include Left Turns—10 minutes
2. Walk through without dogs and run Course #102-2L—30 minutes
3. Teach Moving Side-step right, Moving Down, Call Front–4 fronts, Halt, Walk Around Dog, and Halt Down Walk Around Dog—10 minutes
4. Review by using Rally signs as Flash cards—10 minutes

Week 5

1. Distribute Exhibitor sheets and do walk-through for Course #N105 — 15 minutes
2. Students run Course #N105 and get scored — 30 minutes
3 Teach some Advanced course signs (students do these on lead): Pivots, Offset Figure 8, Halt, Call Front and Finish (stationary), Backing, as for Excellent — 15 minutes

Week 6

Reminder: Advanced and Excellent must be <u>Off Lead</u> in competition.

1. Teach correct jumping technique (on lead) for future Advanced and Excellent courses
2. Distribute Exhibitor Sheets and do walk-through without dogs for Course #A105
3. Students run this course ON LEAD to review previous week's advanced turns and sign recognition
4. Review working as a team, talking to dogs, watching numbers, keeping it fun, and keeping everything smooth and easy on the specator's eye
5. Congratulations on their first Rally experience.

Rally ON!

Lesson 1
Right Turns

I am a firm believer in teaching turns one direction at a time. I want to make sure that the dog and the handler thoroughly understand and can execute a turn in one direction before teaching a turn in the opposite direction. This avoids "turn" confusion for both parts of the team and helps to perfect each turn separately.

This chapter consists of two Right Turn Courses to use when teaching the Right Turn signs. You want to instill visual recognition on the handler's part. Later there are additional, advanced Right Turn exercises that utilize the basics learned on these courses.

Course #101-1R is designed as a basic Right Turns Only course. Normal heeling is stressed between exercises. You want to establish a smooth rhythm to the dog and handler teamwork. Concentrate on smooth, even turns as you train.

Course #101-2R is designed with Right Turns Only, but with change of pace heeling.

Except for those signs indicating a change of direction—Right Turn, or 270° Right—all signs are placed to the *right* of the handler's path. Signs indicating a change of direction are placed *directly in front* of the handler.

These courses are also designed to help the handler get a feel for where he or she needs to execute the exercise in relation to the placement of the sign, i.e., how much space will be needed to do the exercise correctly? (This depends to some extent on the size of the dog.)

You must execute the moving (heeling) exercises about 1 1/2 feet in front of and to the left of the sign. This way the handlers can see the signs as they are doing the exercises. Teach them to take the time to read the sign again! ALL turn signs will be directly in front of the handler's path of travel. Turn exercises must be executed directly in FRONT of the sign, not next to it.

I've started this book with Right Turns. Although I recommend training only one direction at a time, you can start with either turn, right or left. The key is to have the handler and dog team master one direction before teaching the other.

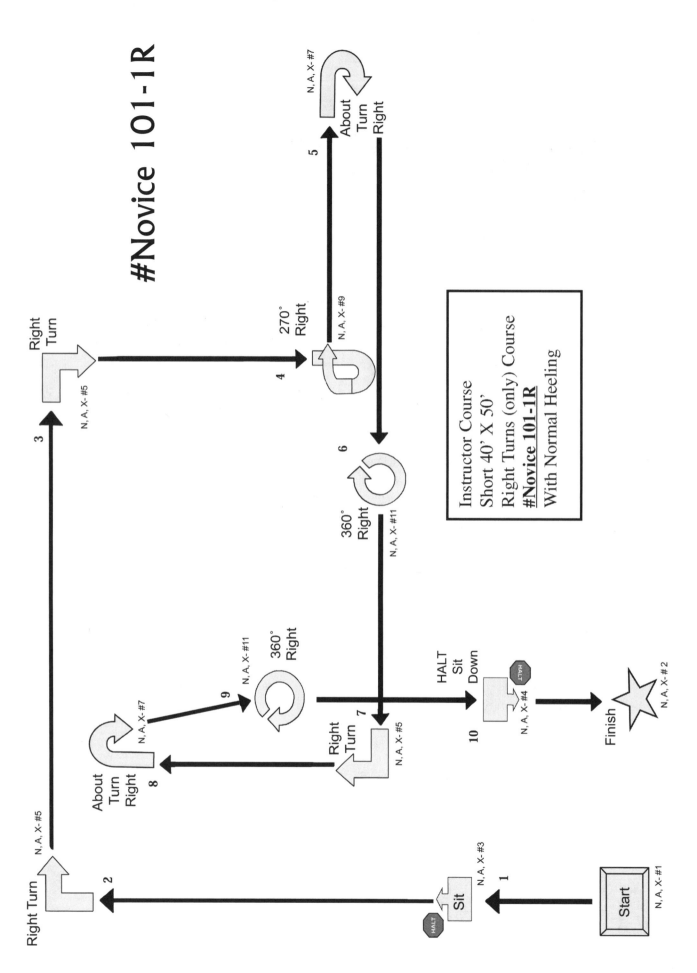

#Novice 101-1R

Right Turn
3
N, A, X- #5

270°
Right
4
N, A, X- #9

**About
Turn
Right**
5
N, A, X- #7

Instructor Course
Short 40' X 50'
Right Turns (only) Course
#Novice 101-1R
With Normal Heeling

6
360°
Right
N, A, X- #11

**About
Turn
Right**
8
N, A, X- #7

360°
Right
9
N, A, X- #11

**Right
Turn**
7
N, A, X- #5

**HALT
Sit
Down**
10
HALT
N, A, X- #4

Finish
N, A, X- #2

Right Turn
2
N, A, X- #5

Sit
1
HALT
N, A, X- #3

Start
N, A, X- #1

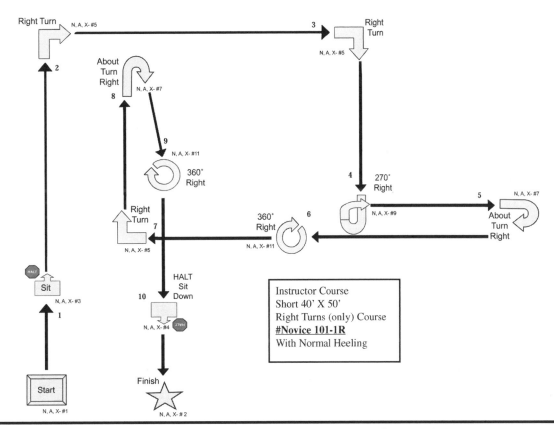

Instructor Course
Short 40' X 50'
Right Turns (only) Course
#Novice 101-1R
With Normal Heeling

Rally Course #Novice 101-1R

This is a Right Turns only course with Normal Heeling. Novice courses MUST be on-lead.

	AKC Rally Sign Numbers
START	1
1. Halt, Sit	3
2. Right Turn	5
3. Right Turn	5
4. 270° Right	9
5. About Turn Right	7
6. 360° Right	11
7. Right Turn	5
8. About Turn Right	7
9. 360° Right	11
10. HALT, Sit Down	4
FINISH	2

NOTE: This is NOT a regulation course setup; practice course only.

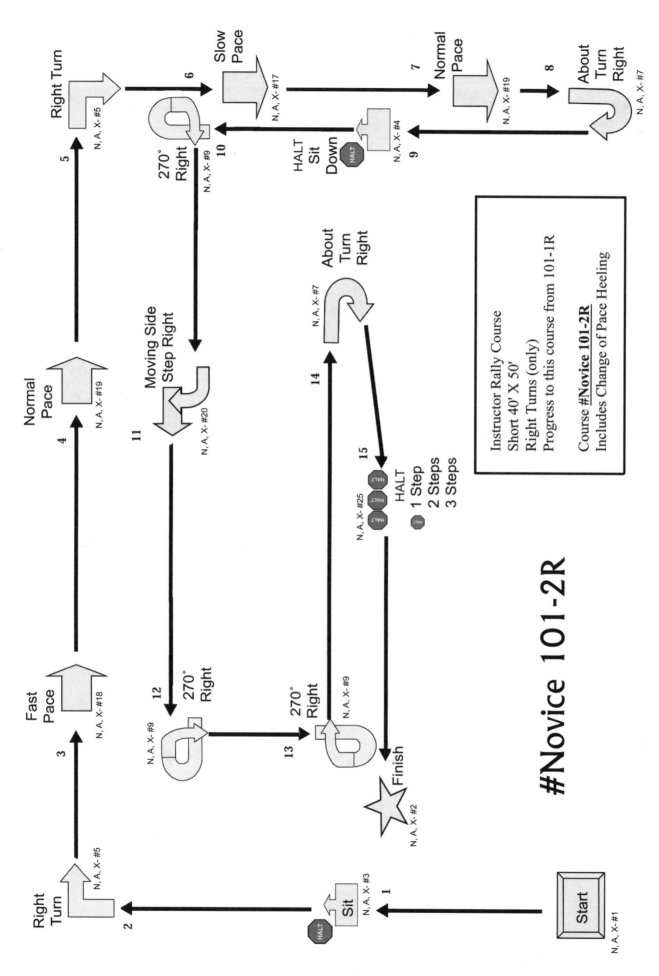

#Novice 101-2R

Instructor Rally Course
Short 40' X 50'
Right Turns (only)
Progress to this course from 101-1R

Course #Novice 101-2R
Includes Change of Pace Heeling

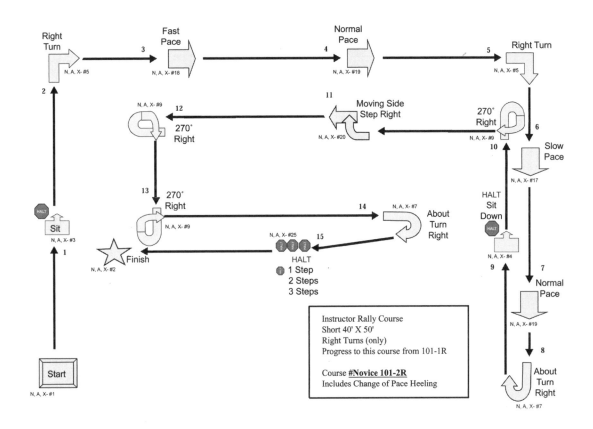

Rally Course #Novice 101-2R

	AKC Rally Sign Numbers
START	1
1. Halt, Sit	3
2. Right Turn	5
3. Fast	18
4. Normal	19
5. Right Turn	5
6. Slow	17
7. Normal	19
8. About Turn Right	7
9. HALT, Sit, Down	4
10. 270° Right	9
11. Moving Side Step Right	20
12. 270° Right	9
13. 270° Right	9
14. About Turn Right	7
15. HALT, 1 step halt, 2 steps halt, 3 steps halt	25
FINISH	2

NOTE: This is NOT a regulation course setup; practice course only.

Lesson 2
Left Turns

Courses #102-1L and #102-2L are Left Turn Only courses. Once again, be sure the left turn has been mastered before doing these courses. When I'm training or judging Left Turns, I look for the dog's head to remain somewhere in the area of the knee, or slightly behind it. Even though heel position in Rally is much more lenient, there are reasons why we train the dog to stay next to us. If the dog forges ahead on a left turn it will impede the handler's forward motion.

Course #102-2L once again adds change of pace heeling. Be careful of where you start your change of pace and where you go back to normal. You don't want to be too far back from the sign in either case. Try to stay within the 1 1/2 foot parameter mentioned in Lesson 1. This rule applies anytime you're moving by a sign, as opposed to changing direction. Again in this course, ALL Left Turn signs will be directly in front of the handler/dog team. Remember: Turns should be executed in FRONT of the sign.

A quick note about change of pace heeling. Establish a rhythm in normal heeling. Handlers should maintain that "length of stride" and just slow forward body motion for the SLOW. They should not change the way they step or their length of stride. They should run in the same "length of stride" for the FAST. This keeps the dog more tuned in.

Once you've completed the Turn courses, you're ready to begin training or practicing the Advanced Rally turn signs. Continue practicing heeling between signs and above all, the handlers should always "talk to their dog." That's the very best part of training for Rally.

#Novice 102-1L

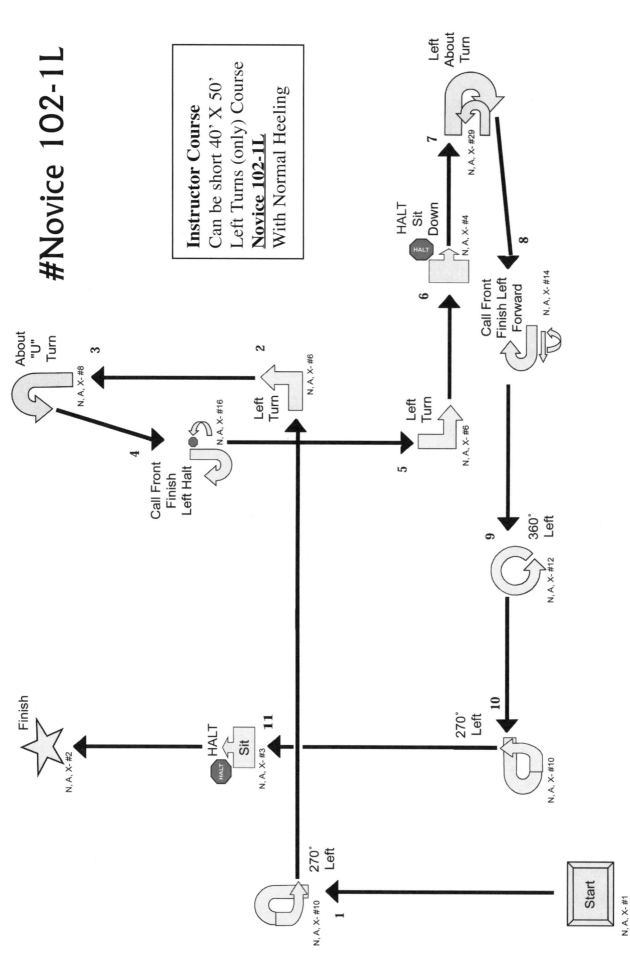

Instructor Course
Can be short 40' X 50'
Left Turns (only) Course
Novice 102-1L
With Normal Heeling

About "U" Turn
3
N, A, X- #8

Left Turn
2
N, A, X- #6

Call Front Finish Left Halt
4
N, A, X- #16

Left About Turn
7
N, A, X- #29

HALT Sit Down
6
N, A, X- #4

Call Front Finish Left Forward
8
N, A, X- #14

Left Turn
5
N, A, X- #6

360° Left
9
N, A, X- #12

270° Left
10
N, A, X- #10

Finish
N, A, X- #2

HALT Sit
11
N, A, X- #3

270° Left
1
N, A, X- #10

Start
N, A, X- #1

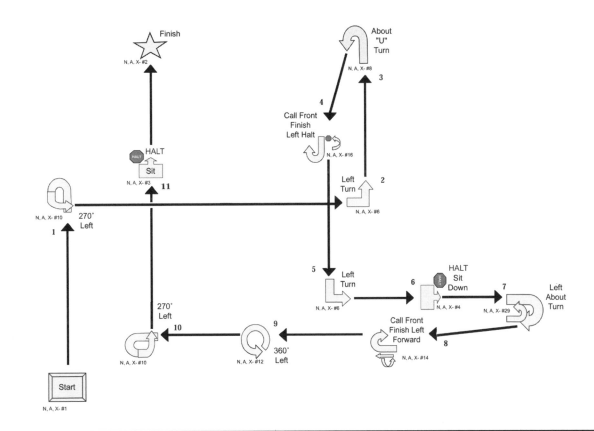

Rally Course #Novice 102-1L

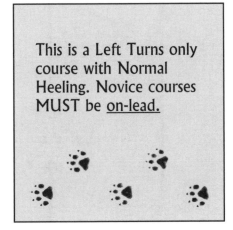

This is a Left Turns only course with Normal Heeling. Novice courses MUST be on-lead.

	AKC Rally Sign Numbers
START	1
1. 270° Left	10
2. Left Turn	6
3. About "U" Turn	8
4. Call Front, Finish Left, HALT	16
5. Left Turn	6
6. HALT, Sit, Down	4
7. Left About Turn	29
8. Call Front, Finish Left, Forward	14
9. 360° Left	12
10. 270° Left	10
11. HALT, Sit	3
FINISH	2

NOTE: This is NOT a regulation course setup; practice course only.

#Novice 102-2L

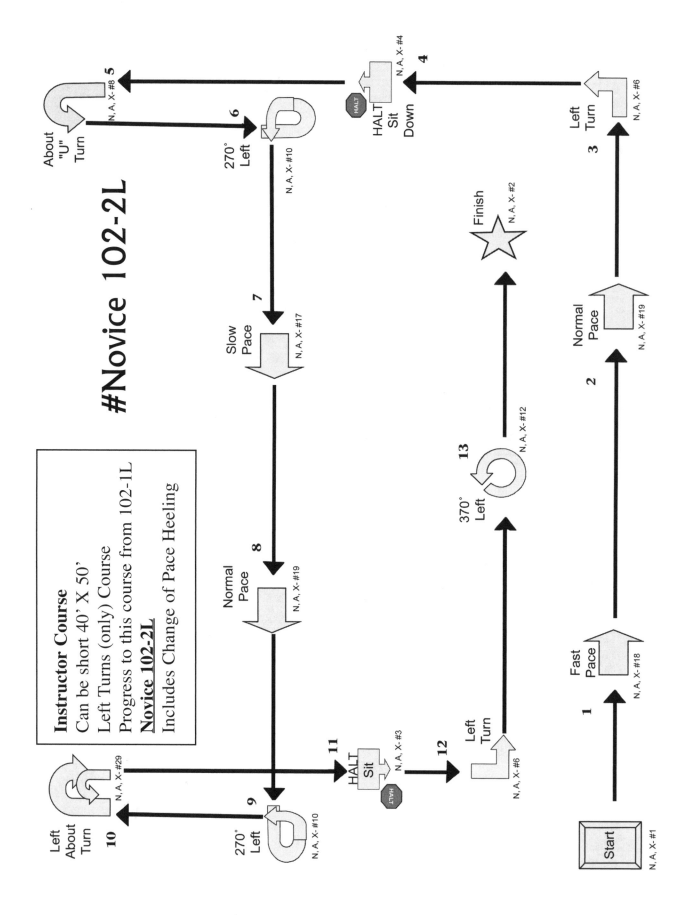

Instructor Course
Can be short 40' X 50'
Left Turns (only) Course
Progress to this course from 102-1L
Novice 102-2L
Includes Change of Pace Heeling

About "U" Turn **5** N, A, X- #8

About "U" Turn **6** 270° Left N, A, X- #10

HALT Sit Down N, A, X- #4 **4**

Left Turn **3** N, A, X- #6

Finish N, A, X- #2

Slow Pace **7** N, A, X- #17

Normal Pace **2** N, A, X- #19

Normal Pace **8** N, A, X- #19

370° Left **13** N, A, X- #12

Fast Pace **1** N, A, X- #18

Left About Turn **10** N, A, X- #29

270° Left **9** N, A, X- #10

HALT Sit **11** N, A, X- #3

Left Turn **12** N, A, X- #6

Start N, A, X- #1

14

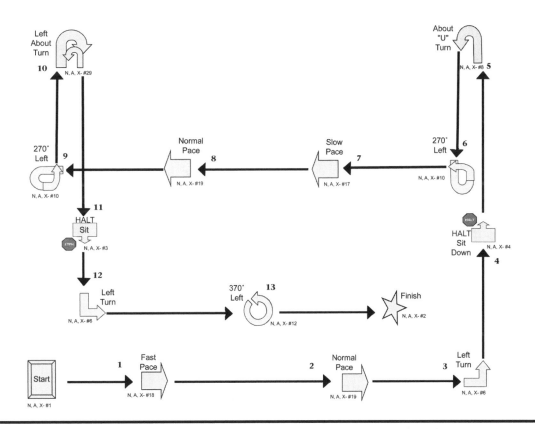

Rally Course #Novice 102-2L

	AKC Rally Sign Numbers
START	1
1. Fast	18
2. Normal	19
3. Left Turn	6
4. HALT, Sit, Down	4
5. About "U" Turn	8
6. 270° Left	10
7. Slow	17
8. Normal	19
9. 270° Left	10
10. Left About Turn	29
11. HALT, Sit	3
12. Left Turn	6
13. 360° Left	12
FINISH	2

NOTE: This is NOT a regulation course setup; practice course only.

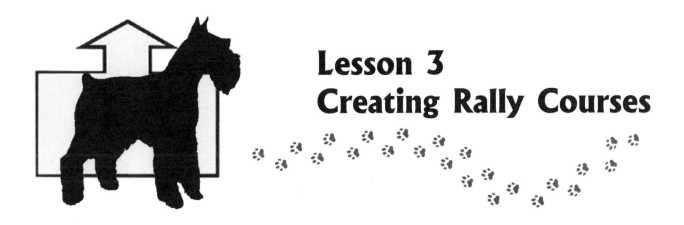

Lesson 3
Creating Rally Courses

The following section is really what this book is all about. I've created posters for you to display outside the Rally ring per AKC rules, and exhibitor sheets to pass out to exhibitors with their armbands. Each course, beginning with Number 103, includes three nested courses: Novice, Advanced, and Excellent.

The full page sheet is the poster. The Exhibitor sheet has a miniaturized copy of the same course at the top, with the stations listed in consecutive order below. Following each station is the AKC sign number on the right side of the sheet. These sign numbers are listed to make it easier for you to pull the signs and place them in correct course order when setting up the course.

AKC Rules/Requirements for Each Level of Rally:

Novice:	10-15 exercises / max 5 stationary	On Lead
Advanced:	12-17 exercises / max 7 stationary	Off Lead
Excellent:	15-20 exercises / max 7 stationary	Off Lead with exception of Honor (On Lead)

General Guidelines for Creating Rally Courses

1. Decide where your entrance will be and design all nested courses to start and finish around the same area.

2. Try to keep to three exercise signs on the short side of any course.

3. There is no specified distance between stations. You must use your own heeling experience as your guide. Allow enough room between cones or stations for a giant dog breed and handler, or a wheelchair team, to work comfortably, keeping their rhythm.

4. Do NOT use any Backing Up exercise as the #1 station.

5. Try to put a Halt exercise as your last station before Finish. This gives the timer steward plenty of time to pick up the stopwatch and be ready to stop the time at the Finish.

6. Allow plenty of room for jumping, about 12 or 15 feet on each side of the jump for safety.

7. Following a jump, the dog is required to return to heel position with the Handler. A moving exercise is much easier to do at the completion of a jump. I prefer any of the following: Moving Down, Call Front (any one of the four exercises numbered 13-16), Straight Figure 8, Serpentine. Avoid using signs with a Halt after a jump. Also try to put jumps in the direction of the long side of the ring. If you must use the short side for a jump, I suggest making it a

Broad Jump. (Remember that a Broad jump can only be approached from one direction.)

8. There are only right-angle turns in Rally. There are no curves or 30-degree turns to help with short or odd angles. Be aware. Coming out of a Right About Turn may need to be off the initial path, depending upon where the next station is placed.

9. Try to put a Halt as your final station before Finish. If you use Fast as a final exercise, it does NOT need a Normal to follow (this only applies to a final exercise on any course). You can also use a Fast Forward from Sit. This, too, does not need a Normal to follow when used as a final exercise.

Creating an Excellent Course

1. Begin with an Excellent Course. It contains the most stations–up to 20.

2. Excellent must have two jumping exercises. The same jump CAN be used twice. All Obedience jumps are permitted; additionally, they CAN be just 4 feet wide, rather than 5 feet wide as required in Obedience. If you use a Broad Jump in Excellent, be aware that Broad jumps can only be approached from one direction. If you decide to use the same jump twice, from different directions, you must use either a High Jump or Bar Jump. Be sure to place at least one station between jumps.

3. In Excellent, don't forget the last numbered station is the Honor exercise. This is done ON leash with the judge announcing prior to the start of the class as to how and where the Honor will be performed in the ring. The judge decides if the handler will be beside or in front of the dog and whether it will be a Long Sit or Long Down as another team performs the course at the same time. A steward will watch the honoring team for infractions. When the judge releases the Honor team at the completion of the exercise, the steward will report to the table steward, who will note the score and time in the judge's book. The judge must always review all scores in the judge's book prior to signing off the book at the end of the class.

4. When using the Offset Figure 8 in Excellent or Advanced, be sure to have covers over food in the bowls. Some dogs may have food allergies and you don't want them to actually be able to get to the food. Toys can be used in place of food. I have extra toys available in case the ones you use have a squeaker and a dog gets a chance to squeak it. You should replace it with another for the next dog. Use cones, or two people can be used as posts (which are the long sides of the Figure 8) about 10 to 12 feet apart, with the distractions (food bowls or toys) on the short sides about 5 or 6 feet apart. These are the distractions that the team passes during the Figure 8. When designing an Offset Figure 8, you MUST show the entrance and exit points of this exercise on your course sheet. The Offset Figure 8 is the only cone exercise that can be entered and exited from any direction. It must fall into the flow of your course direction.

5. You can utilize cones in several different exercises on one course. Be sure to make a note to the show-giving Rally Chairman as to how many cones you'll need for each course. The largest number in any one course is sufficient for the club to supply.

6. Exercise Sign numbers 46 through 50 are for Excellent only. Signs numbered 1 through 50 are all allowed in Excellent courses.

Guidelines for Creating Advanced Courses

1. Signs numbered 1 through 45 can be used for Advanced.

2. All previous information regarding jumps, the Offset Figure 8, and distances for jumps and

between stations apply to these courses also.

3. Advanced uses ONE JUMP, and it can be any one of the Obedience jumps as before.

4. Be sure to count your stationary exercises when you complete your course. Remember, you may have no more than 7 stationary exercises in Advanced. Also be aware that all Call Front exercises are considered to be stationary exercises. Even though these exercises don't always show a HALT sign, they are still considered stationary by the AKC. Moving Down, Moving Stand, and Walk Around Dog are also stationary.

5. Start by eliminating all "Excellent only" signs from the course. Replace them as closely as possible with the signs already in place. Be sure to check the numbers for the stations and set up the changes as closely as possible to the already numbered locations. There are fewer signs/stations in Advanced, so some renumbering will be required in this course as well as in Novice courses.

Guidelines for Creating Novice Courses

1. Only signs numbered 1 through 31 can be used in Novice.

2. Remember to allow plenty of room between stations for heeling and for the execution of each station.

3. Eliminate all but the allowed Novice signs and replace them as closely as possible with something similar in execution. Only 10 to 15 stations are permitted in Novice, so more numbers will be removed.

4. Up to 5 Stationary exercises are permitted in Novice. Be sure to count them. This includes Call Front exercises and the Moving Down as above.

Suggestions for Preparing for a Rally Judging Assignment

Be sure you have a signed contract from the club that hires you. This should include your charges and expenses, e.g., travel and meals.

Get a Rally contact name and address from the Club. This person should be able to tell you what size ring you will have. You can then pick your courses ahead of time and send the exhibitor sheets to this person 1 to 2 weeks ahead of the day of the show to have copies made.

When I send my sheets for copies, I attach a sticky note with things like: "Need 1 broad jump, 1 high or bar jump. Will need a total of 9 cones. Need 2 food dishes with covers. Need food for the bowls."

Be sure the club or Superintendent for the show has all the equipment, signs, numbers, etc., before you leave your home. I always carry extras of the most common signs in my briefcase, such as: Right Turn, Left Turn, About Turn. (These have an asterisk in the sign listings in this book.)

I always carry two stopwatches in case the club doesn't have their own. I carry my own work/score sheets and final sheet for listing scores, and tape for hanging course posters. I prefer to use a pencil on my score sheets in case I need to make a correction, so I also carry a small pencil sharpener.

These are but a few suggestions. Have a good time, and fill your briefcase with whatever makes your job simpler and more fun.

Rally Exercises

Novice: 10-15 exercises / max 5 stationary   **Advanced:** 12-17 exercises / max 7 stationary

Excellent: 15-20 exercises / max 7 stationary

N	A	E	Novice, Advanced, Excellent	#
			START	1
			FINISH	2
			HALT–Sit and Forward (S)	3
			HALT–Down Dog and Forward	4
			Right Turn	5
			Left Turn	6
			About Turn Right	7
			About "U" Turn	8
			270° Right Turn	9
			270° Left Turn	10
			360° Right Turn	11
			360° Left Turn	12
			Call Dog Front–Forward Right (S)	13
			Call Dog Front–Forward Left (S)	14
			Call Dog Front–Finish Right (S)	15
			Call Dog Front–Finish Left (S)	16
			Slow Pace	17
			Fast Pace	18
			Normal Pace	19
			Moving Side Step Right	20
			Spiral Right–Dog Outside	21
			Spiral Right–Dog Inside	22
			Straight Figure 8	23
			Serpentine	24
			HALT–1, 2, and 3 Steps Forward (S)	25
			Call Front–1, 2, and 3 Steps Backward (S)	26
			Moving Down–Then Forward (S)	27
			HALT–Fast Forward from Sit (S)	28
			Left About Turn	29
			HALT and Walk Around Dog (S)	30
			HALT, Down–Walk Around Dog (S)	31
	A	E	**Advanced, Excellent**	
			HALT–About Turn Right and Forward (S)	32
			HALT–About Turn Left and Forward (S)	33
			Send Over Jumps–Handler Runs By	34
			HALT–Turn Right One Step–Call to Heel (S)	35
			HALT–Stand Dog–Walk Around (S)	36
			HALT–90° Pivot Right–HALT	37
			HALT–90° Pivot Left–HALT	38
			Offset Figure 8	39
			HALT–Side Step Right (S)	40
			HALT–Call Dog Front–Finish Right and Forward (S)	41
			HALT–Call Dog Front–Finish Left and Forward (S) 42	
			HALT–180° Pivot Right–Halt and Forward (S)	43
			HALT–180° Pivot Left–Halt and Forward (S)	44
		E	HALT, Down, Sit (S)	45
			Excellent	
			HALT, Stand, Down (S)	46
			HALT, Stand, Sit (S)	47
			Moving Stand, Walk around Dog, Forward (S)	48
			Backup 3 Steps	49

AKC Rally Signs With Explanations

The following exercises may be used in all class levels:

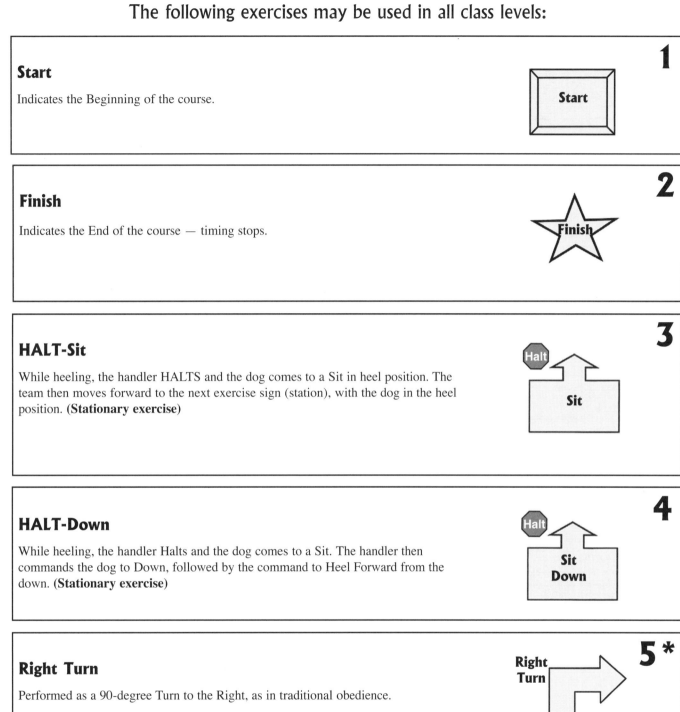

Start

Indicates the Beginning of the course.

1

Finish

Indicates the End of the course — timing stops.

2

HALT-Sit

While heeling, the handler HALTS and the dog comes to a Sit in heel position. The team then moves forward to the next exercise sign (station), with the dog in the heel position. **(Stationary exercise)**

3

HALT-Down

While heeling, the handler Halts and the dog comes to a Sit. The handler then commands the dog to Down, followed by the command to Heel Forward from the down. **(Stationary exercise)**

4

Right Turn

Performed as a 90-degree Turn to the Right, as in traditional obedience.

5 *

Left Turn

Performed as a 90-degree Turn to the Left, as in traditional obedience.

6 *

*Indicates sign may be duplicated

7*  About Turn–Right

While heeling, the team makes a 180-degree About Turn to the handler's Right.

8*  About "U" Turn

While heeling, the team makes a 180-degree About Turn to the handler's Left.

9*  270° Right Turn

While heeling, the team makes a 270-degree turn to the handler's right. 270-degree turns are performed as a tight circle, but *not* around the exercise sign.

10*  270° Left Turn

While heeling, the team makes a 270-degree turn to the handler's left. 270-degree turns are performed as a tight circle, but *not* around the exercise sign.

11 360° Right Turn

While heeling, the team makes a 360-degree turn (a complete circle) to the handler's right. 360-degree turns are performed as a tight circle, but *not* around the exercise sign.

12 360° Left Turn

While heeling, the team makes a 360-degree turn (a complete circle) to the handler's left. 360-degree turns are performed as a tight circle, but *not* around the exercise sign.

*Indicates sign may be duplicated

Call Dog Front–Forward Right

While heeling, the handler stops his/her forward motion and calls the dog to the Front position (the dog sits in front and faces the handler). The handler may take several steps backward as the dog turns and moves to a Sit in the Front position. The second part of the exercise directs the handler to move forward while commanding the dog to change from the Front position to the handler's right, around behind the handler, and into Heel position as the handler continues forward. The dog does not sit before heeling Forward in heel position with the handler. (**Stationary exercise**)

13

Call Front Finish Right Forward

Call Dog Front–Forward Left

While heeling, the handler stops his/her forward motion and calls the dog to the Front position (the dog sits in front and faces the handler). The handler may take several steps backward as the dog turns and moves to Sit in the Front position. The second part of the exercise directs the handler to move forward while commanding the dog to change from the front position to the handler's left, moving into Heel position as the handler continues forward. The dog does not sit before moving forward at heel position with the handler. (**Stationary exercise**)

14

Call Front Finish Left Forward

Call Dog Front–Finish Right–HALT

While heeling, the handler stops his/her forward motion and calls the dog to the front position (dog sits in front and faces the handler). The handler may take several steps backward as the dog turns and moves to a Sit in the Front position. The second part is the Finish to the Right where the dog must return to the heel position by moving around the right of the handler. Dog must Sit in heel position before moving forward in heel position with the handler. (**Stationary exercise**)

15

Call Front Finish Right HALT

Call Dog Front–Finish Left–HALT

While heeling, the handler stops his/her forward motion and calls the dog to the front position (dog sits in front and faces the handler). The handler may take several steps backward as the dog turns and moves to Sit in the Front position. The second part is the Finish to the Left, where the dog must move to the handler's left and Sit in heel position. Dog must Sit in the heel position before moving forward in heel position with the handler. (**Stationary exercise**)

16

Call Front Finish Left HALT

Slow Pace

Dog and handler must Slow down noticeably. Must be followed by Normal Pace unless it is at the end of the stations for the class.

17*

Slow Pace

Fast Pace

Dog and handler must speed up noticeably. Must be followed by Normal Pace unless it is at the end of the stations for the class.

18*

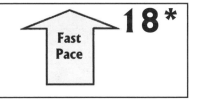

Fast Pace

*Indicates sign may be duplicated

19* Normal Pace

Dog and handler must move forward showing willingness and enjoyment, while walking briskly and naturally.

20  Moving Side Step Right

While heeling, the handler takes one step diagonally to the right and continues, moving forward along the newly established line. The dog maintains heel position.

21  Spiral Right–Dog Outside

This exercise requires three pylons or posts placed in a straight line with space between them of approximately 6-8 feet. Spiral Right indicates the handler must turn to the right when moving around each pylon or post. This places the dog on the *outside* of the turns. The approach, spiral patterns and directions of exits are illustrated on the course map with arrows indicating the path of the team. The exercise sign is placed near or on the first pylon or post where the spiral is started.

22  Spiral Left–Dog Inside

This exercise requires three pylons or posts placed in a straight line with spaces between them of approximately 6-8 feet. Spiral Left indicates the handler must turn to the left when moving around each pylon or post. This places the dog in the *inside* of the turns. The approach, spiral patterns and direction of exit are illustrated on the course map with arrows indicating the path of the team. The exercise sign is placed near or on the first pylon or post where the spiral is started.

23 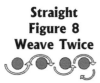 Straight Figure 8

This exercise requires four obstacles (pylons, posts or people) placed in a straight line with spaces between them of approximately 6-8 feet. The exercise sign is placed near or on the first obstacle in the series (this could be at either end, depending on the approach from the previous exercise). Entry into the weaving pattern is with the first obstacle at the dog/handler's *left* side. The dog and handler circle the end obstacle and return, weaving once in each direction.

24  Serpentine

This exercise requires four obstacles (pylons, posts or people) placed in a straight line with spaces between them of approximately 6-8 feet. The exercise sign is placed near or on the first obstacle in the series (this could be at either end, depending on the approach from the previous exercise). Entry into the weaving pattern is with the first obstacle at the dog/handler's left side. It should be noted that in this exercise the team does *not* return as they do in the Straight Figure 8, but weaves in one direction only and continues in the same direction as they were going originally.

*Indicates sign may be duplicated

HALT–1, 2, 3 Steps Forward

25

The team halts with the dog sitting in heel position. The handler takes one step forward with the dog in heel position, and halts. The dog sits. This is followed by two steps and a halt, and then three steps forward and halt. The dog heels each time the handler moves forward and sits each time the handler halts. **(Stationary exercise)**

Call Dog Front–1, 2, 3 Steps Backward

26

While heeling, the handler stops forward motion and calls dog to the Front position. The handler may take several steps backward as the dog turns and moves to a Sit in the Front position. With the dog in the Front position, the handler takes one step backward and halts. This is followed by two steps and halt, and three steps and halt. Each time, the dog moves with the handler and resumes a Sit in the front position as the handler halts. Handler then commands dog to resume heel position as the team moves forward to the next station. **(Stationary exercise)**

Moving Down–Then Forward

27

While moving forward with the dog in heel position, the handler commands the dog to drop into a down position and pauses next to the dog. Once the dog is completely in the down position, the handler moves forward, commanding the dog to heel. **(Stationary exercise)**

HALT–Fast Forward from Sit

28

With the dog Sitting in heel position, the handler commands the dog to Heel and immediately moves forward at a fast pace. This exercise must be followed by a normal pace, or it may be placed as the last exercise on the course, in which case the exercise and performance are concluded as the team crosses the finish line. **(Stationary exercise)**

Left About Turn

29

While moving with the dog in heel position, the handler makes an about turn to the left. At the same time, the dog must move around the handler's right and back into Heel position. The dog does *not sit* before moving forward in heel position with the handler.

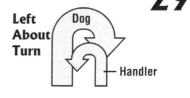

HALT and Walk Around Dog

30

With dog Sitting in heel position, the handler commands the dog to stay and proceeds to walk around the dog to the left, returning to Heel position. The handler should pause in heel position before moving forward to the next station. **(Stationary exercise)**

31

HALT–Down–Walk Around Dog

With dog sitting in heel position, the handler commands the dog to Down and Stay. Handler then proceeds to walk around the dog to the left, returning to heel position. The handler should pause in heel position before moving forward to the next station. **(Stationary exercise)**

The following exercises may be used in Advanced and Excellent classes only:

32

HALT–About Turn Right and Forward

With the dog Sitting in the heel position, the handler turns 180° to the right and immediately moves forward without halting. **(Stationary exercise)**

33

HALT–About "U" Turn and Forward

With the dog Sitting in the heel position, the handler turns 180° to the left and immediately moves forward without halting. **(Stationary exercise)**

34*

Send Over Jump – Handler Runs By

While moving with the dog in heel position, the handler directs the dog to take the jump as the handler runs by it. When the dog has completed the jump, it is called to heel position and the team continues to the next exercise.

35

HALT–Turn Right One Step–Call to Heel (HALT)

With the dog Sitting in heel position, the handler commands the dog to wait or stay. The handler then pivots to the right while taking one step in that direction, and Halts. The dog is called to sit at heel position in the new location before moving forward to the next station. Note: This is the <u>only</u> exercise in which the dog does <u>not move</u> with the handler, but <u>stays</u> instead. **(Stationary exercise)**

*Indicates sign may be duplicated

HALT–Stand Dog–Walk Around

With the dog Sitting in heel position, the handler will Stand the dog, command him to Stay, leave and walk around the dog to the left, returning to heel position. The handler should pause in heel position before moving forward to the next station. In the Advanced Class, the handler may touch the dog, move forward to stand the dog, and may pose the dog as in the show ring. (**Stationary exercise**)

HALT–90° Pivot Right–HALT and Forward

With the dog Sitting in the heel position, the team pivots 90° to the right, and halts. The dog sits. Then the team moves forward (**Stationary exercise**)

HALT–90° Pivot Left–HALT and Forward

With the dog Sitting in heel position, the team pivots 90° to the left, and halts. The dog sits. Then the team moves forward. (**Stationary exercise**)

Off-Set Figure 8

This exercise requires two pylons, posts or people placed about 8-10 feet apart around which the team will perform a complete Figure 8. Two distractions will be arranged to the sides of the Figure 8, about 5-6 feet apart. Entry may be between the pylons, posts or people and the distraction on either side. The distractions will consist of two loosely covered – but secure – containers with tempting dog treats; however, dog toys may replace one or both containers, or may be placed next to the containers. Arrows will illustrate the approaches, weaving pattern and exit of the team.

HALT–Side Step Right–HALT

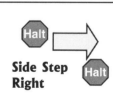

With the dog Sitting in the heel position, the team moves one step directly to the right and halts. The dog moves *with* the handler and Sits in Heel position when the handler halts. (**Stationary exercise**)

HALT–Call Dog Front–Finish Right and Forward

With the dog Sitting in heel position, the handler calls the dog to Front. On command, the dog then moves from the Front position around the right of the handler and Sits in heel position. Handler may *not* step backward to aid dog during exercise. (**Stationary exercise**)

42

Call Dog Front Finish Left

HALT–Call Dog Front–Finish Left and Forward

With the dog Sitting in heel position, the handler calls the dog to Front. On command, the dog then moves from the Front position to the handler's left and Sits in heel position. Handler may *not* step backward to aid dog during exercise. **(Stationary exercise)**

43

180° Pivot Right

HALT–180° Pivot Right–Halt and Forward

With the dog Sitting in heel position, the team pivots 180° in place to the right. The dog moves with the handler and sits in the heel position. The team then moves forward. **(Stationary exercise)**

44

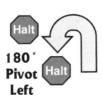

180° Pivot Left

HALT–180° Pivot Right–HALT

With the dog Sitting in heel position, the team pivots 180° in place to the left. The dog moves with the handler and sits in the heel position. **(Stationary exercise)**

45

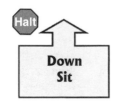

Down Sit

HALT–Down–Sit

With dog Sitting in heel position, the handler commands the dog to Down, then to Sit. **(Stationary exercise)**

The following exercises may be used in Excellent classes only:

46

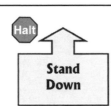

Stand Down

HALT–Stand–Down

With the dog Sitting in heel position, the handler will Stand the dog (without physical handling), then command the dog to Down. The handler then commands the dog to heel forward from the Down position. **(Stationary exercise)**

47

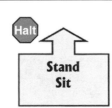

Stand Sit

HALT–Stand–Sit

With the dog Sitting in heel position, the handler will command the dog to Stand without touching the dog, then command the dog to Sit. **(Stationary exercise)**

Moving Stand–Walk Around Dog–Forward

While Heeling and with no hesitation, the handler will Stand the dog, leave and walk around the dog to the left, returning to heel position. The handler should pause in heel position before moving forward to the next station. **(Stationary exercise)**

48

Backup 3 Steps

While heeling, the handler reverses direction, walking backward 3 steps without first halting, and then continues heeling forward. The dog moves backward with the handler and maintains heel position throughout the exercise without sitting.

49

Honor Exercise

This exercise will be performed on a leash. Dog and handler can enter through the exit gate, or may proceed directly to the Honor Station after completing the Excellent Course. The judge will designate whether the dog is to perform a sit-stay or a down-stay. This shall be for the duration of time it takes for the next dog to run the entire course. The judge will also designate whether the handler is to stand next to the dog or facing the dog at the end of the leash during the Honor exercise. All dogs in the class must perform the exercise in the same manner. The Honor dog will be monitored and scored by a steward, as directed by the judge.

Honor

50

Some General Regulations

- Heel from sign to sign in a continuous performance. Handlers may praise their dogs and give repeated commands and signals.

- Novice is done on leash. Advanced and Excellent are done off leash.

- Scoring: The team starts with 100 points. Qualifying performance is 70 and successful completion of each exercise. The heeling from sign to sign is judged. Minimum deduction is one point.

- Jump heights: Under 15 inches – Jump 8 inches; 15 to less than 20 inches – Jump 12 inches; 20 inches or more – Jump 16 inches.

- Broad jump: Cover a distance equal to twice the height of the high jump setting for each dog. Three hurdles are used for distances of 28-32 inches and 2 hurdles for distances of 16-24 inches.

Glossary of Terms

Brisk, briskly – keenly alive, alert, energetic

Command – verbal order from handler to dog

Gently – with kindness, without harshness or roughness

Natural – not artificial; free of affectation, and customarily expected in the home or public places

Order – direction from judge to handler

Signal – nonverbal direction from the handler to dog

Withers – highest point of the dog's shoulder

90°, 180° – pivots performed in place

270°, 360° – turns performed as a tight circle

Halt – dog must sit in heel position

Lack of control – dog is temporarily distracted but returns to working as a team and completes the course

Unmanageable – dog not under control and does not work as a team

Front – dog must sit in front of and facing handler

Section 2

Rally Courses
and Exhibitor Sheets

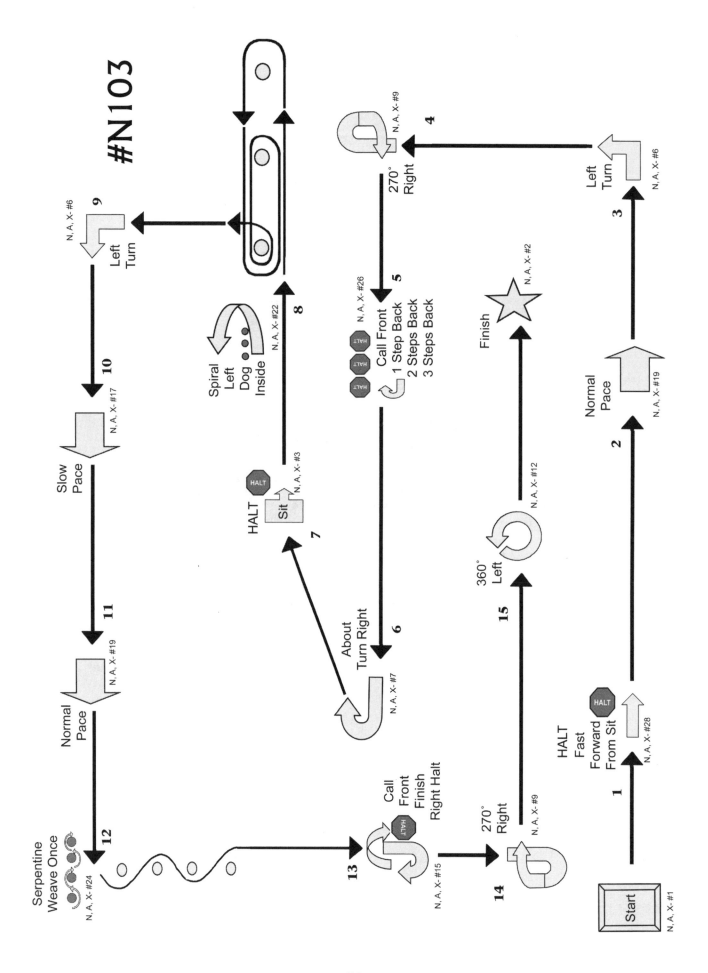

#N103

32

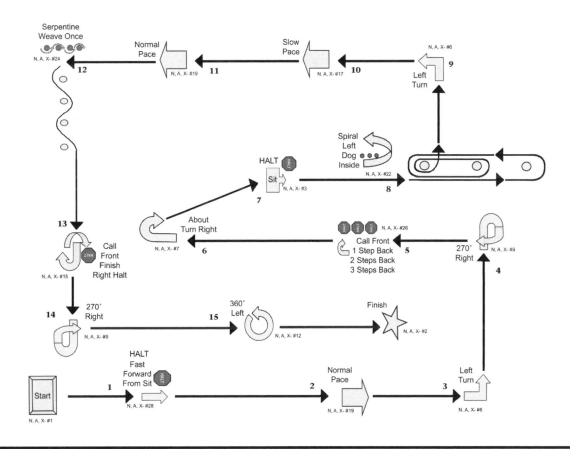

Rally Course #N103

Order of Exercises	AKC Rally Sign Numbers
START	1
1. HALT, Fast Forward From Sit	28
2. Normal	19
3. Left Turn	6
4. 270° Right	9
5. Call Front, 1 Step, 2 Steps, 3 Steps Back	26
6. About Turn Right	7
7. HALT, Sit	3
8. Spiral Left, Dog Inside	22
9. Left Turn	6
10. Slow	17
11. Normal	19
12. Serpentine	24
13. Call Front, Finish Right	15
14. 270° Right	9
15. 360° Left	12
FINISH	2

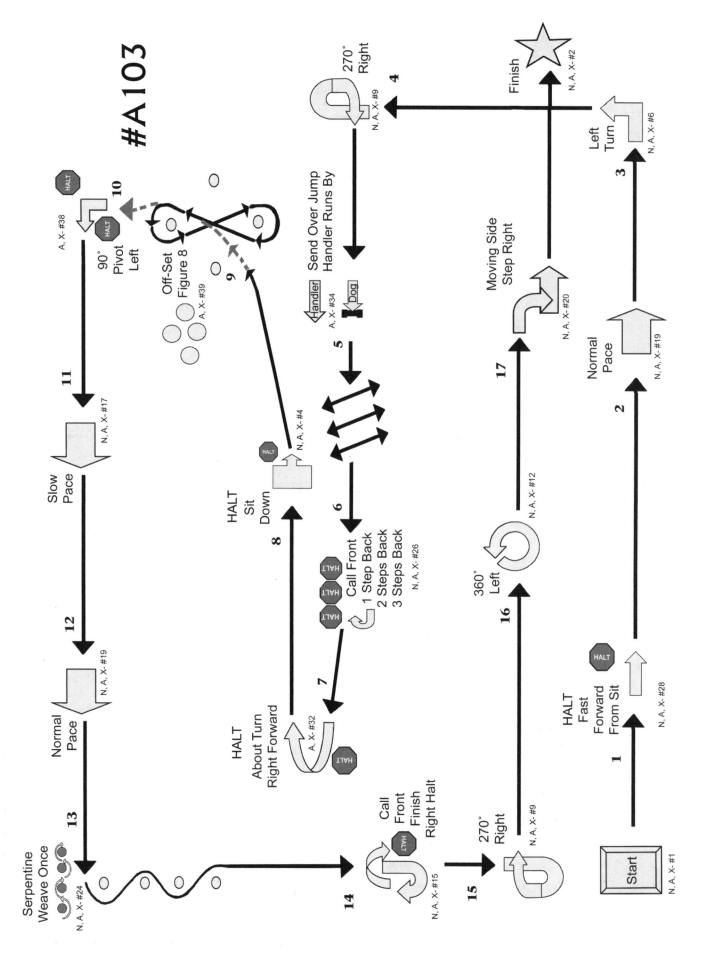

#A103

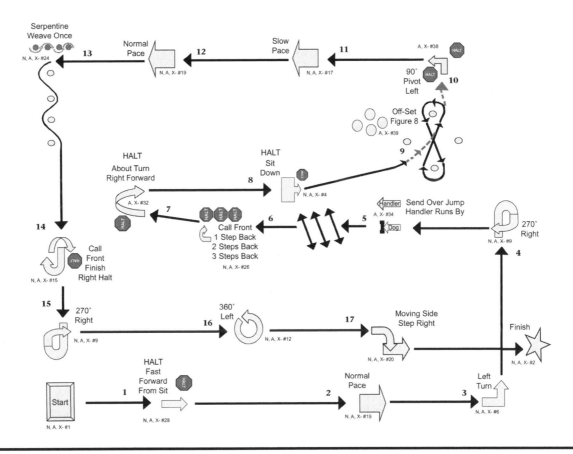

Rally Course #A103

Order of Exercises	AKC Rally Sign Numbers
START	1
1. HALT, Fast Forward From Sit	28
2. Normal	19
3. Left Turn	6
4. 270° Right	9
5. Send Over Jump, Handler Runs By	34
6. Call Front, 1 Step, 2 Steps, 3 Steps Back	26
7. HALT, About Turn Right Forward	32
8. HALT, (sit) Down	4
9. Off Set Figure 8	39
10. HALT, 90° Pivot Left, HALT	38
11. Slow	17
12. Normal	19
13. Serpentine	24
14. Call Front, Finish Right, HALT	15
15. 270° Right	9
16. 360° Left	12
17. Moving Side Step Right	20
FINISH	2

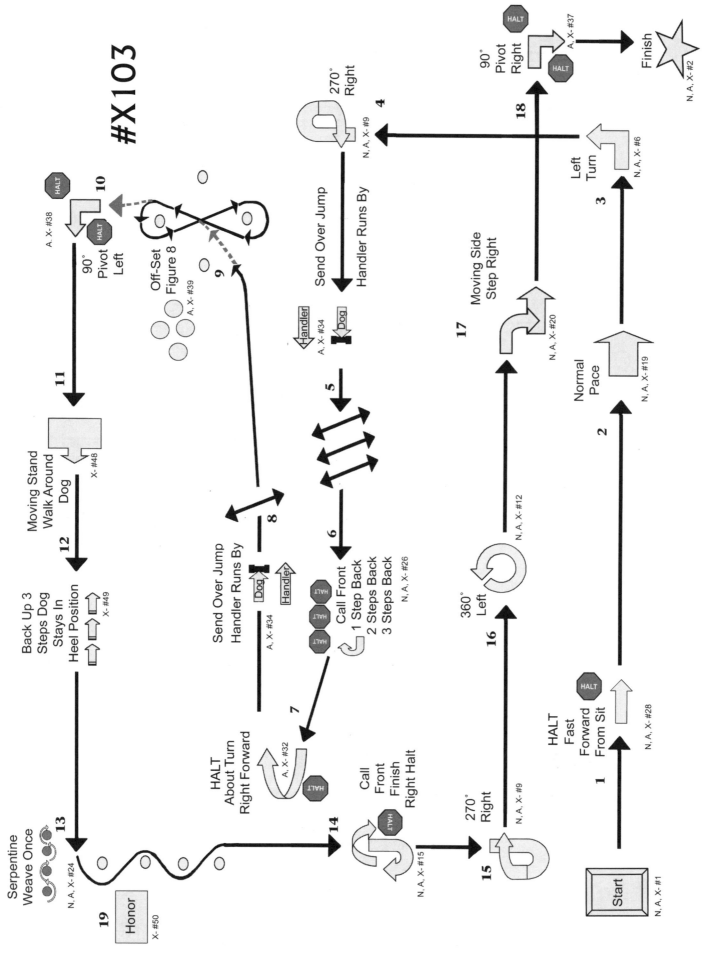

#X103

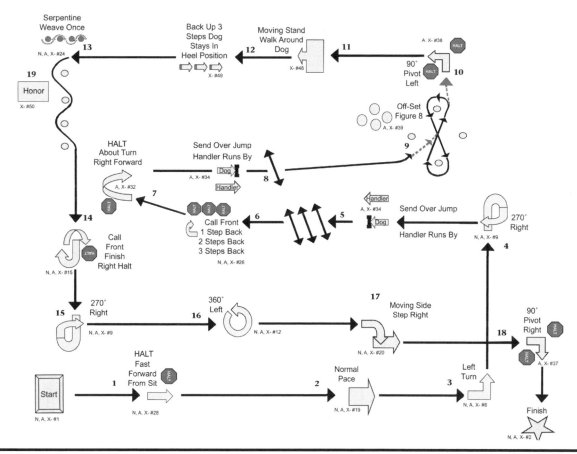

Rally Course #X103

Order of Exercises	AKC Rally Sign Numbers
START	1
1. HALT, Fast Forward From Sit	28
2. Normal	19
3. Left Turn	6
4. 270° Right	9
5. Send Over Jump, Handler Runs By	34
6. Call Front, 1 Step, 2 Steps, 3 Steps Back	26
7. HALT, About Turn Right Forward	32
8. Send Over Jump, Handler Runs By	34
9. Off Set Figure 8	39
10. HALT, 90° Pivot Left, HALT	38
11. Moving Stand Walk Around Dog	48
12. Backup 3 Steps, Dog stays at Heel	49
13. Serpentine	24
14. Call Front, Finish Right, HALT	15
15. 270° Right	9
16. 360° Left	12
17. Moving Side Step Right	20
18. HALT, 90° Pivot right, HALT	37
FINISH	2
19. HONOR	50

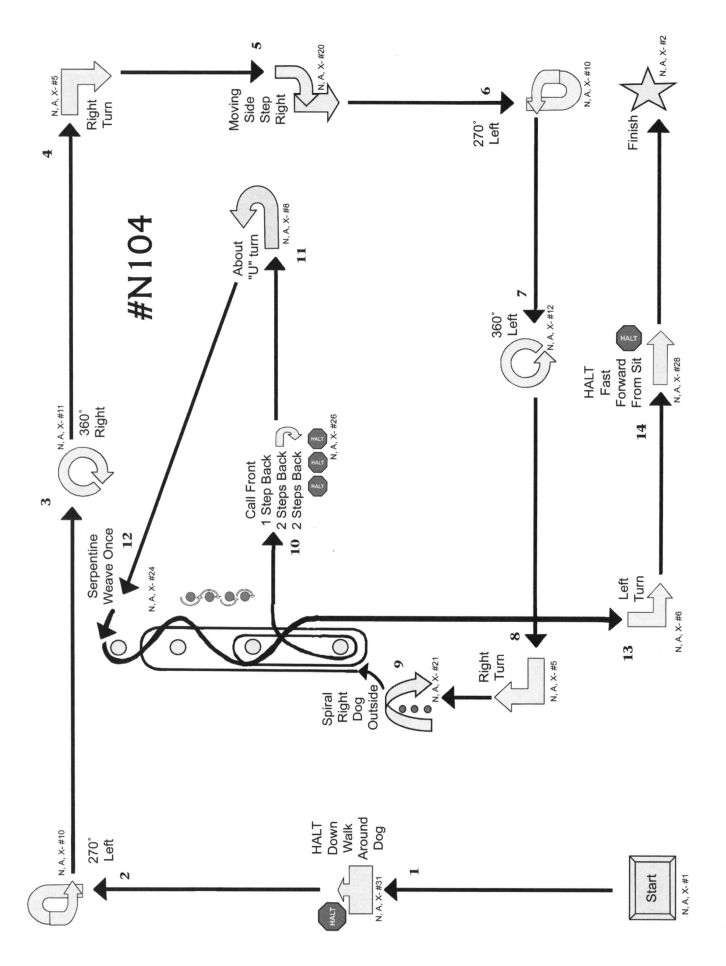

#N104

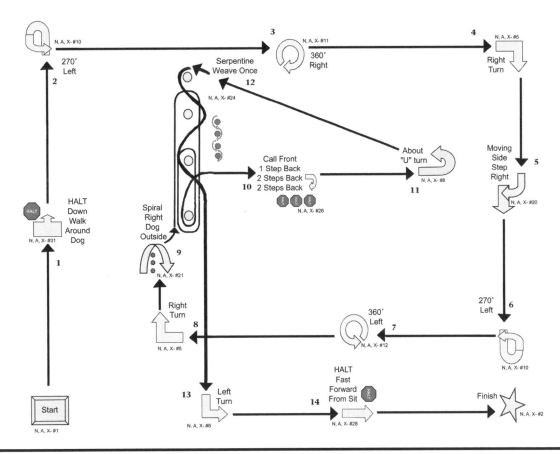

Rally Course #N104

Order of Exercises	AKC Rally Sign Numbers
START	1
1. HALT, Down Walk Around Dog	31
2. 270° Left	10
3. 360° Right	11
4. Right Turn	5
5. Moving Side Step Right	20
6. 270° Left	10
7. 360° Left	12
8. Right Turn	5
9. Spiral Right, Dog Outside	21
10. Call Front, 1 Step, 2 Steps, 3 Steps Back	26
11. About "U" Turn	8
12. Serpentine	24
13. Left Turn	6
14. HALT, Fast Forward from Sit	28
FINISH	2

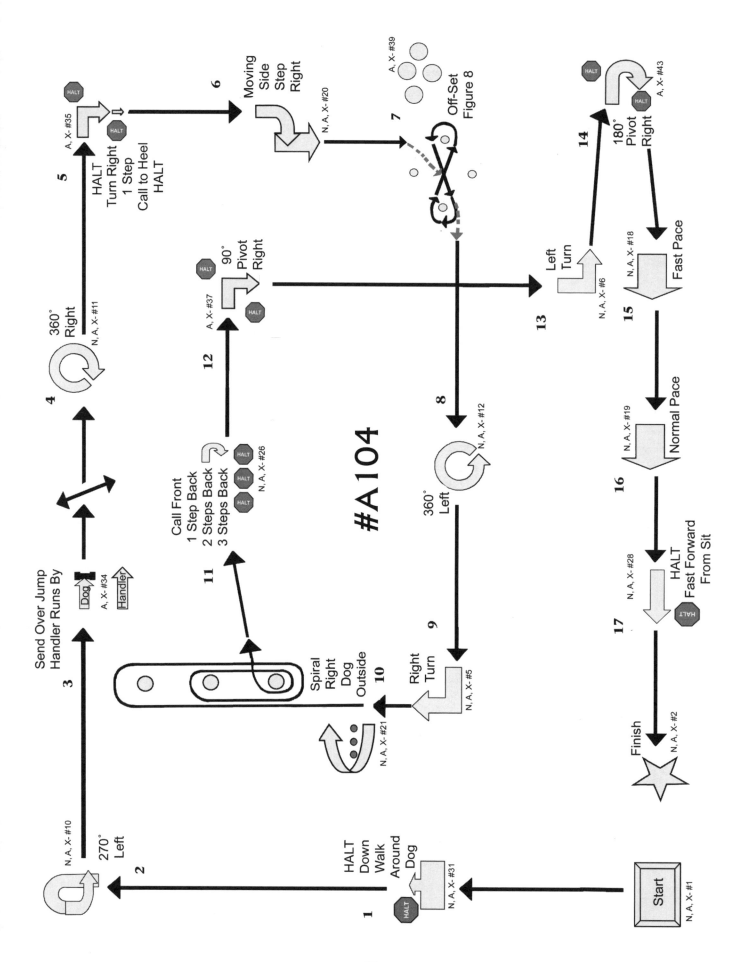

#A104

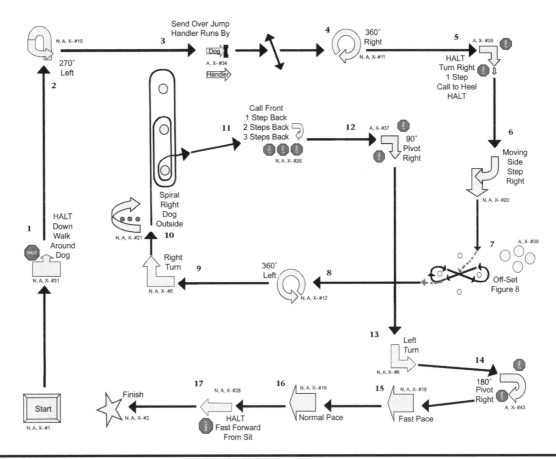

Rally Course #A104

Order of Exercises

	AKC Rally Sign Numbers
START	1
1. HALT, Down, Walk Around Dog	31
2. 270° Left	9
3. Send Over Jump, Handler Runs By	34
4. 360° Right	11
5. Halt, Turn Right, One Step, Call to Heel	35
6. Moving Side Step Right	20
7. Off Set Figure 8	39
8. 360° Left	12
9. Right Turn	5
10. Spiral Right, Dog Outside	21
11. Call Front, 1 Step, 2 Steps, 3 Steps Back	26
12. Halt, 90° Pivot Right, Halt	37
13. Left Turn	6
14. Halt, 180° Pivot Right, Halt	43
15. Fast	18
16. Normal	19
17. Halt, Fast Forward From Sit	28
FINISH	2

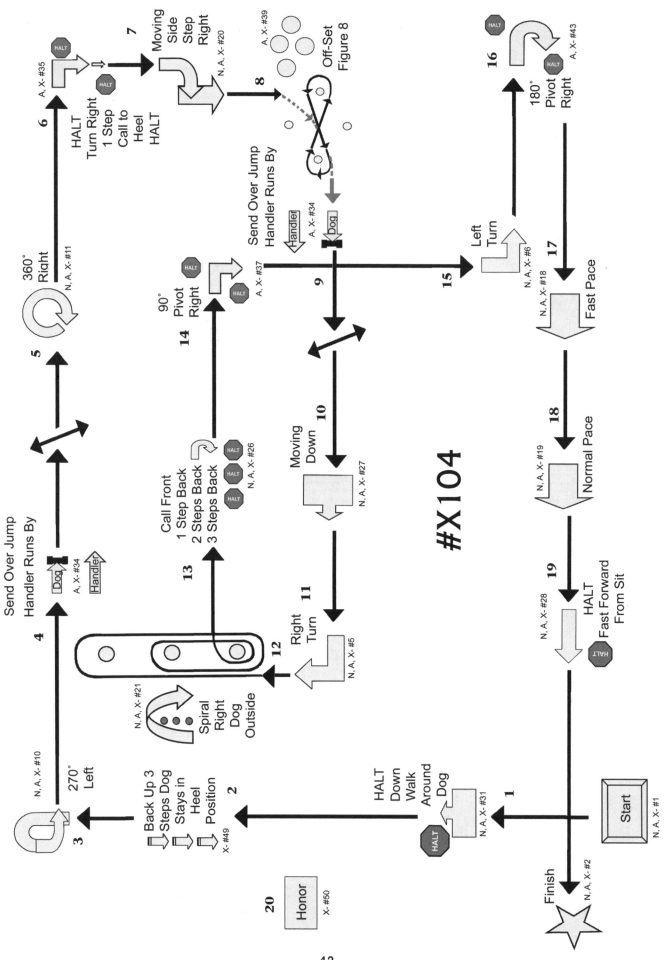

#X104

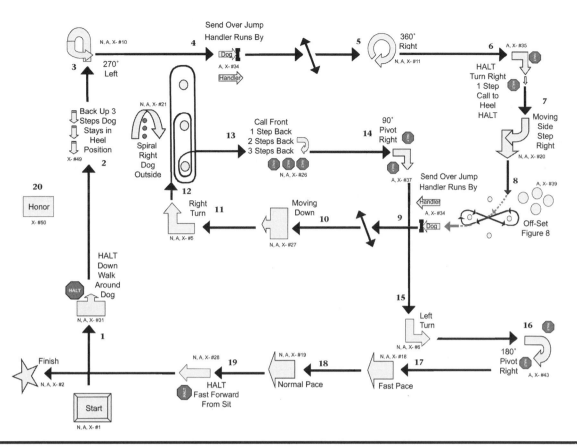

Rally Course #X104

Order of Exercises	AKC Rally Sign Numbers
START	1
1. HALT, Down, Walk Around Dog	31
2. Back up 3 Steps, Dog remains at Heel	49
3. 270° Left	9
4. Send Over Jump, Handler Runs By	34
5. 360° Right	11
6. Halt, Turn Right, 1 Step, Call to Heel, Halt	35
7. Moving Side Step Right	20
8. Off Set Figure 8	39
9. Send Over Jump, Handler Runs By	34
10. Moving Down	27
11. Right Turn	5
12. Spiral Right, Dog Outside	21
13. Call Front, 1 Step, 2 Steps, 3 Steps Back	26
14. Halt, 90° Pivot Right, Halt	37
15. Left Turn	6
16. Halt, 180° Right, Halt	43
17. Fast	18
18. Normal	19
19. Halt, Fast Forward from Sit	28
FINISH	2
20. HONOR	50

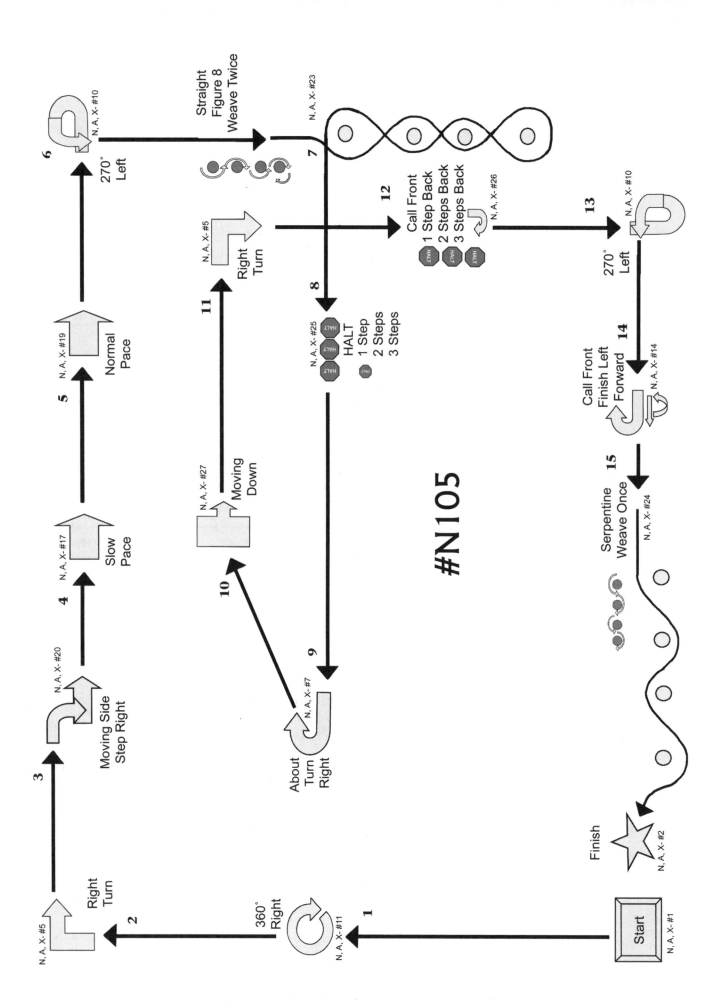

#N105

6
270° Left
N, A, X- #10

Straight
Figure 8
Weave Twice
N, A, X- #23

7

5
Normal
Pace
N, A, X- #19

12
Call Front
1 Step Back
2 Steps Back
3 Steps Back
N, A, X- #26

13
270° Left
N, A, X- #10

4
Slow
Pace
N, A, X- #17

11
Right
Turn
N, A, X- #5

8
HALT
1 Step
2 Steps
3 Steps
N, A, X- #25

14
Call Front
Finish Left
Forward
N, A, X- #14

3
Moving Side
Step Right
N, A, X- #20

10
Moving
Down
N, A, X- #27

15
Serpentine
Weave Once
N, A, X- #24

9
About
Turn
Right
N, A, X- #7

Finish
N, A, X- #2

2
Right
Turn
N, A, X- #5

360°
Right
N, A, X- #11

1
Start
N, A, X- #1

44

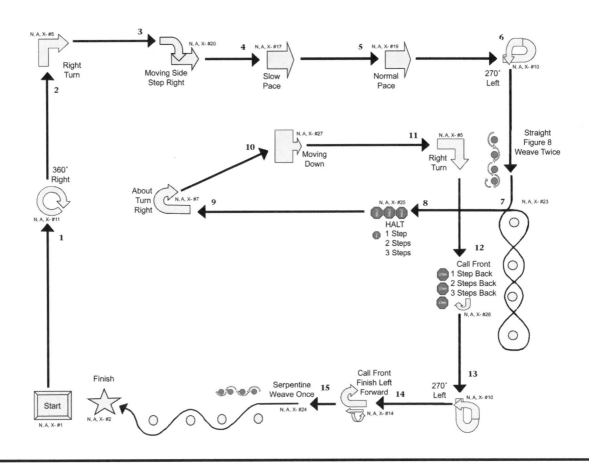

Rally Course #N105

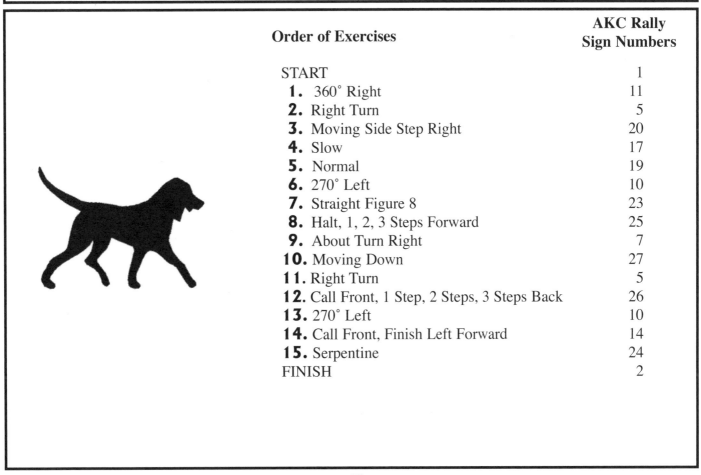

Order of Exercises	AKC Rally Sign Numbers
START	1
1. 360° Right	11
2. Right Turn	5
3. Moving Side Step Right	20
4. Slow	17
5. Normal	19
6. 270° Left	10
7. Straight Figure 8	23
8. Halt, 1, 2, 3 Steps Forward	25
9. About Turn Right	7
10. Moving Down	27
11. Right Turn	5
12. Call Front, 1 Step, 2 Steps, 3 Steps Back	26
13. 270° Left	10
14. Call Front, Finish Left Forward	14
15. Serpentine	24
FINISH	2

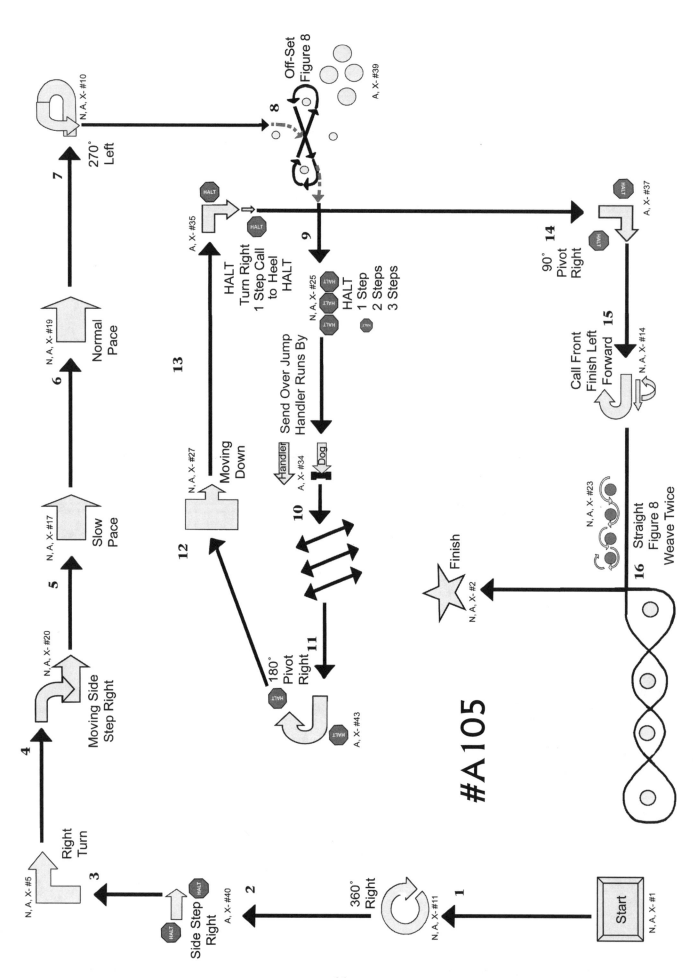

#A105

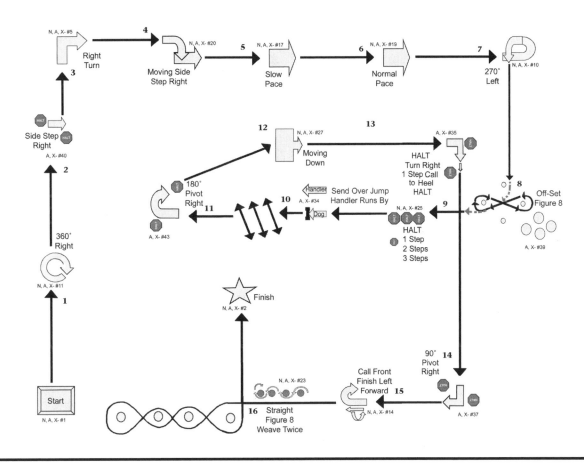

Rally Course #A105

Order of Exercises	AKC Rally Sign Numbers
START	1
1. 360° Right	11
2. Halt, Side Step Right, Halt	40
3. Right Turn	5
4. Moving Side Step Right	20
5. Slow	17
6. Normal	19
7. 270° Left	10
8. Off Set Figure 8	39
9. Halt, 1, 2, 3, Steps Forward	25
10. Send Over Jump, Handler Runs By	34
11. Halt, 180° Pivot Right, Halt	43
12. Moving Down	27
13. Halt, Turn Right One Step, Call to Heel, HALT	35
14. Halt, 90° Pivot Right, Halt	37
15. Call Front Finish Left Forward	14
16. Straight Figure 8	23
FINISH	2

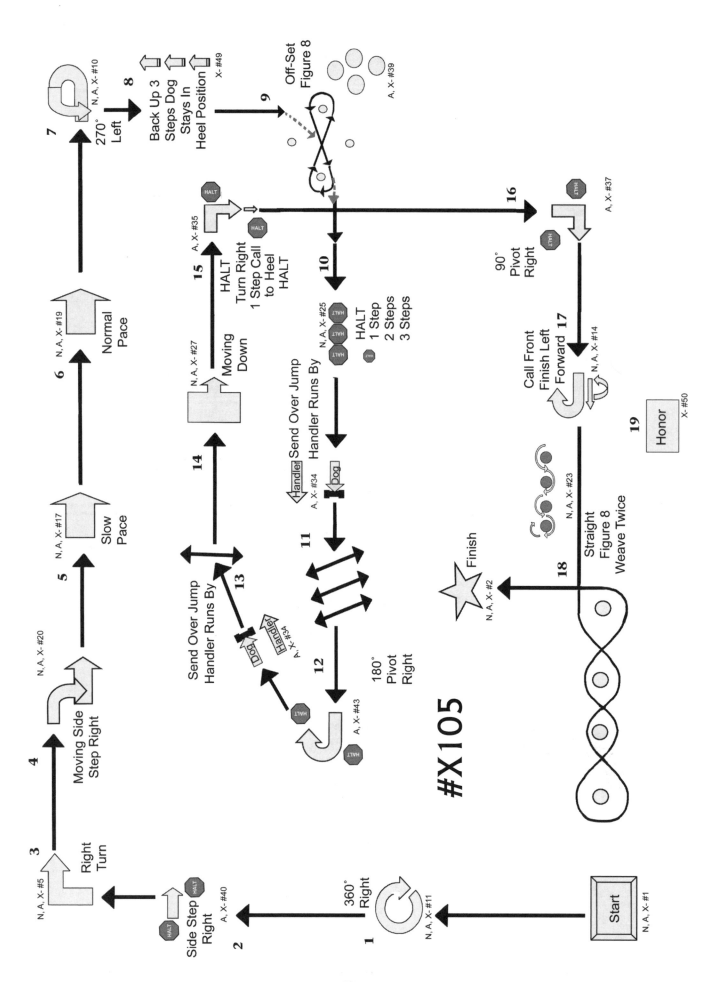

#X105

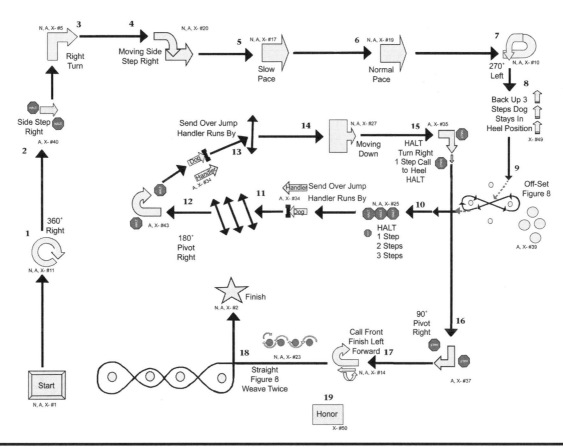

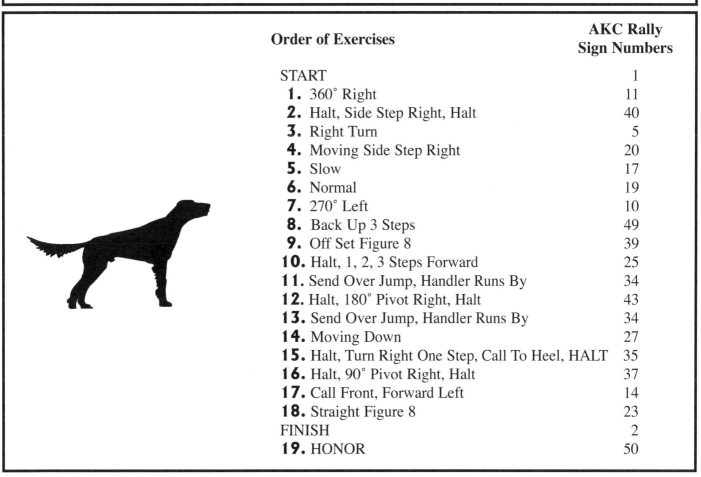

Rally Course #X105

Order of Exercises	AKC Rally Sign Numbers
START	1
1. 360° Right	11
2. Halt, Side Step Right, Halt	40
3. Right Turn	5
4. Moving Side Step Right	20
5. Slow	17
6. Normal	19
7. 270° Left	10
8. Back Up 3 Steps	49
9. Off Set Figure 8	39
10. Halt, 1, 2, 3 Steps Forward	25
11. Send Over Jump, Handler Runs By	34
12. Halt, 180° Pivot Right, Halt	43
13. Send Over Jump, Handler Runs By	34
14. Moving Down	27
15. Halt, Turn Right One Step, Call To Heel, HALT	35
16. Halt, 90° Pivot Right, Halt	37
17. Call Front, Forward Left	14
18. Straight Figure 8	23
FINISH	2
19. HONOR	50

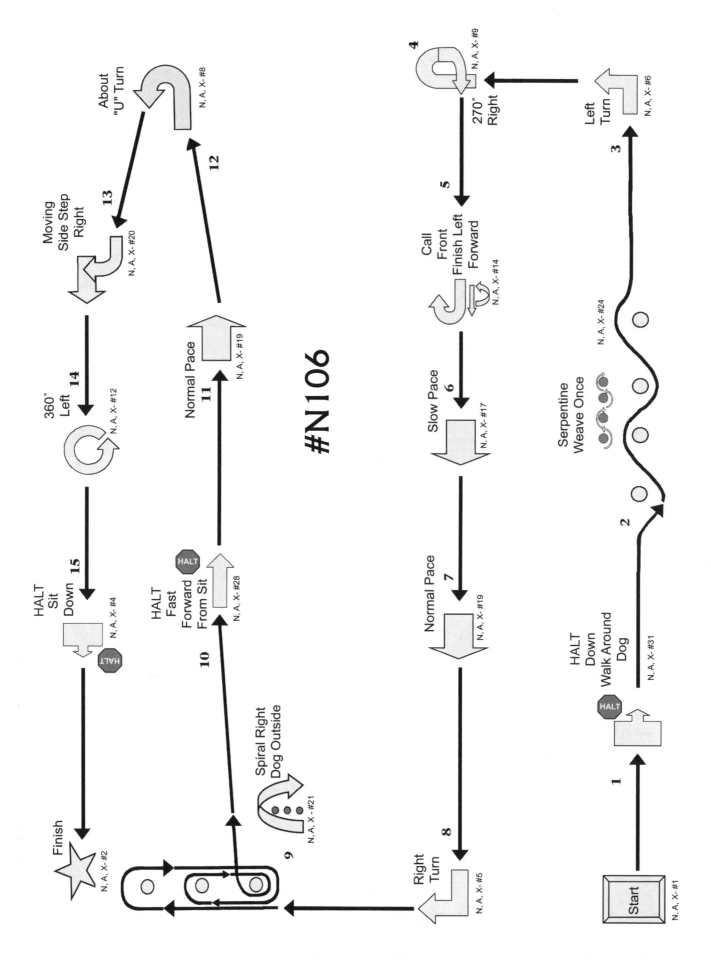

#N106

50

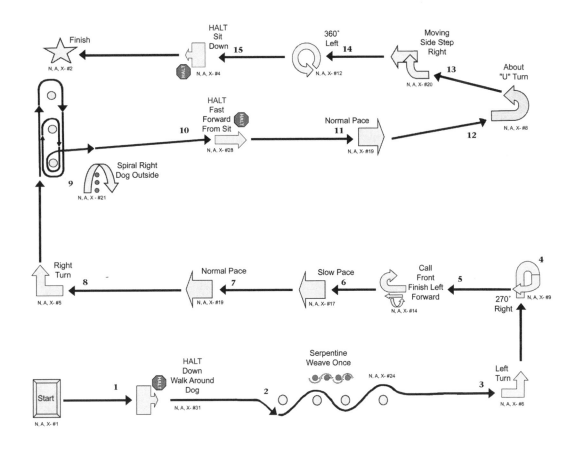

Rally Course #N106

Order of Exercises	AKC Rally Sign Numbers
START	1
1. Halt, Down, Walk Around Dog	31
2. Serpentine	24
3. Left Turn	6
4. 270° Right	9
5. Call Front, Finish Left Forward	14
6. Slow	17
7. Normal	19
8. Right Turn	5
9. Spiral Right, Dog on the Outside	21
10. Halt, Fast Forward from Sit	28
11. Normal	19
12. About "U" Turn	8
13. Moving Side Step Right	20
14. 360° Left	12
15. Halt, Sit, Down	4
FINISH	2

#A106

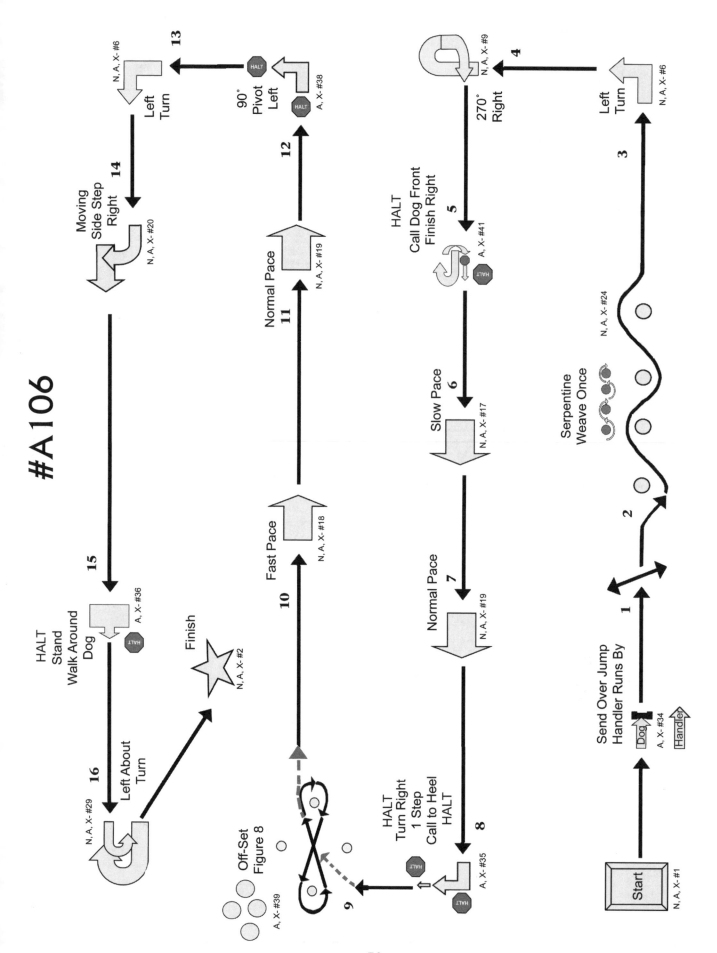

52

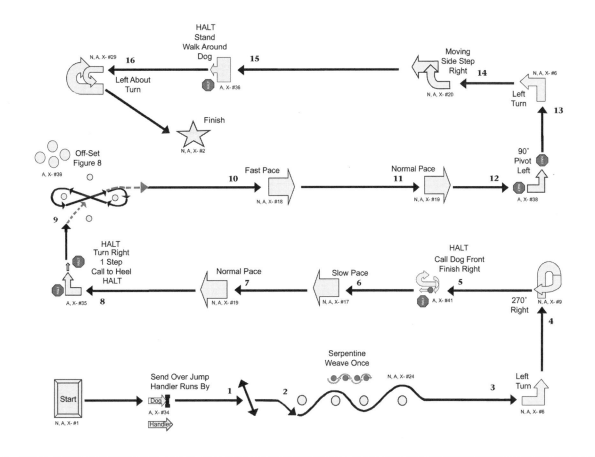

Rally Course #A106

Order of Exercises	AKC Rally Sign Numbers
START	1
1. Send Over Jump, Handler Runs By	34
2. Serpentine	24
3. Left Turn	6
4. 270° Right	9
5. Halt, Call Dog Front, Finish Right, Halt	15
6. Slow	17
7. Normal	19
8. Halt, Turn Right, 1 Step, Call Dog to Heel	35
9. Off Set Figure 8	39
10. Fast	18
11. Normal	19
12. Halt, 90° Pivot Left, Halt	38
13. Left Turn	6
14. Moving Side Step Right	20
15. Halt, Stand, Walk Around Dog	36
16. Left About Turn	29
FINISH	2

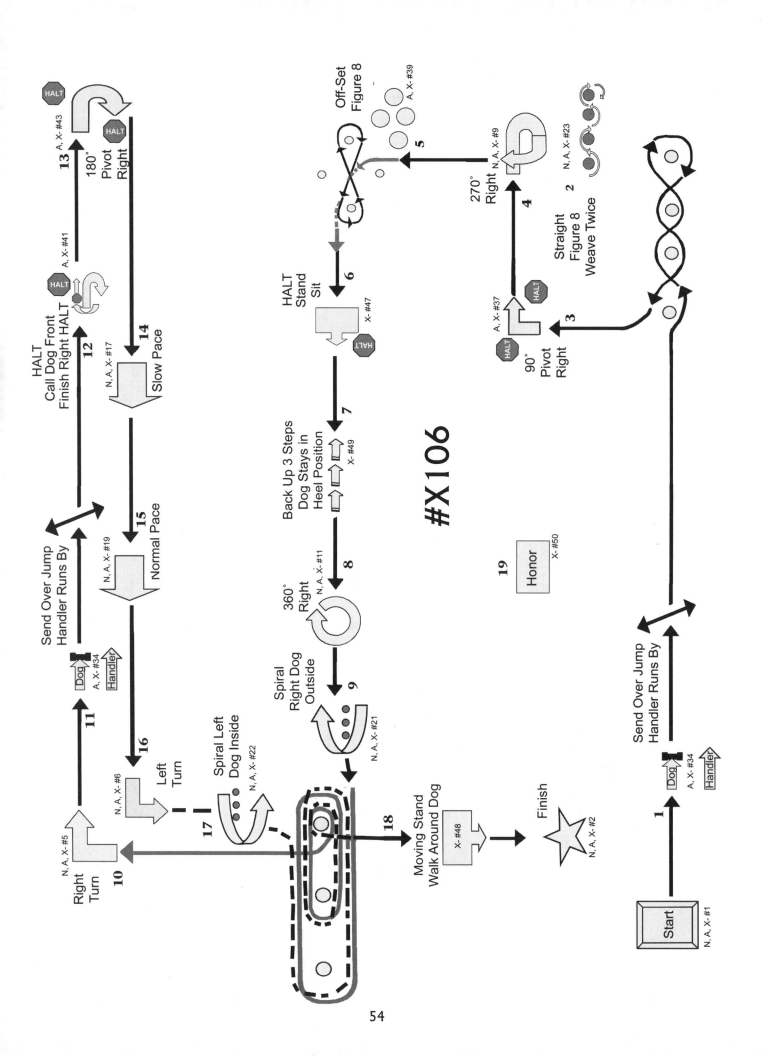

#X106

54

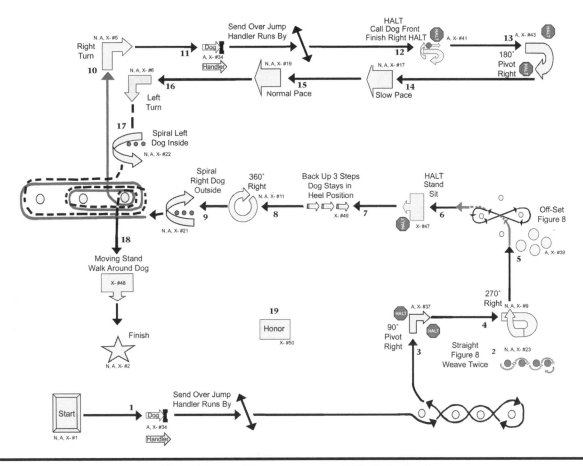

Rally Course #X106

Order of Exercises	AKC Rally Sign Numbers
START	1
1. Send Over Jump, Handler Runs By	34
2. Straight Figure 8	23
3. Halt, 90° Pivot Right, Halt	37
4. 270° Right	9
5. Off Set Figure 8	39
6. Halt, Stand, Sit	47
7. Back up 3 Steps, Dog Stays At Heel	49
8. 360° Right	11
9. Spiral Right, Dog Outside	21
10. Right Turn	5
11. Send Over Jump, Handler Runs By	34
12. Halt, Call Dog Front, Finish Right, Halt	41
13. Halt, 180° Pivot Right, Halt	43
14. Slow	17
15. Normal	19
16. Left Turn	6
17. Spiral Left, Dog Inside	22
18. Moving Stand, Walk Around Dog	48
FINISH	2
19. HONOR	50

#N107

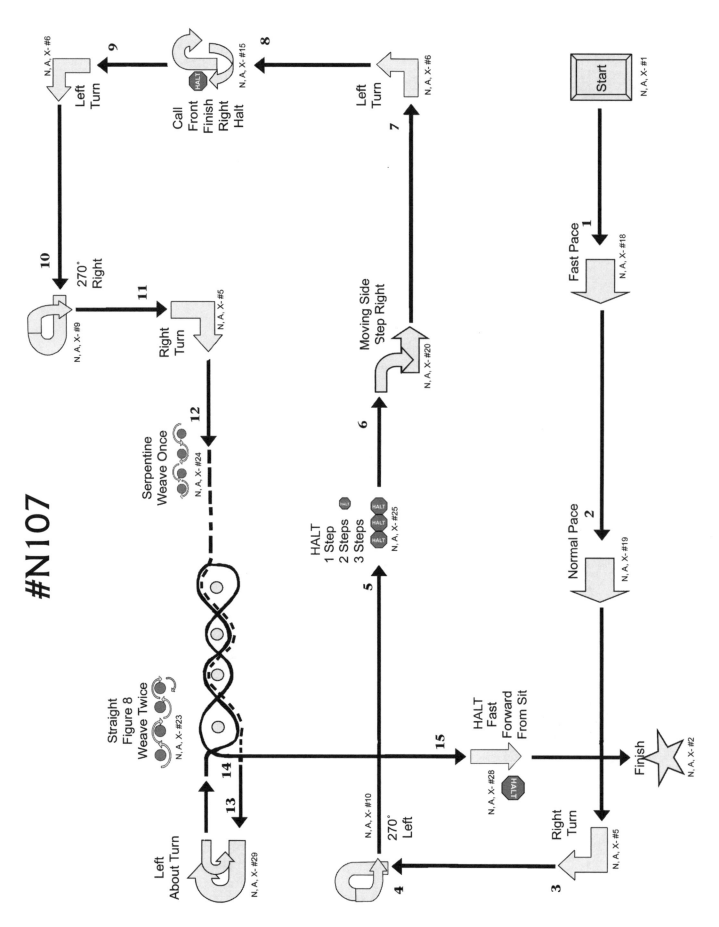

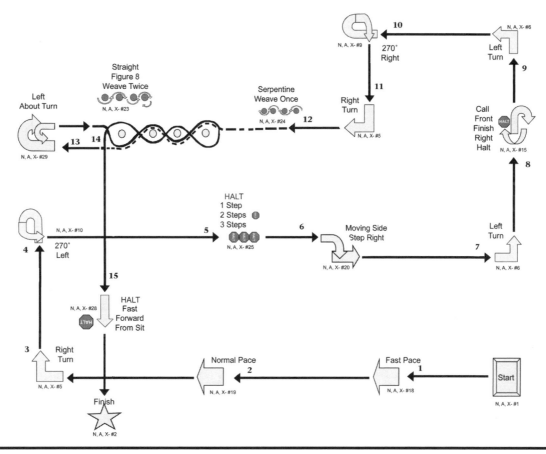

Rally Course #N107

Order of Exercises	AKC Rally Sign Numbers
START	1
1. Fast	18
2. Normal	19
3. Right Turn	5
4. 270° Left	10
5. Halt, 1, 2, 3 Steps Forward	25
6. Moving Side Step Right	20
7. Left Turn	6
8. Call Front, Finish Right, Halt	15
9. Left Turn	6
10. 270° Right	9
11. Right Turn	5
12. Serpentine	24
13. Left About Turn	29
14. Straight Figure 8	23
15. Halt, Fast Forward From Sit	28
FINISH	2

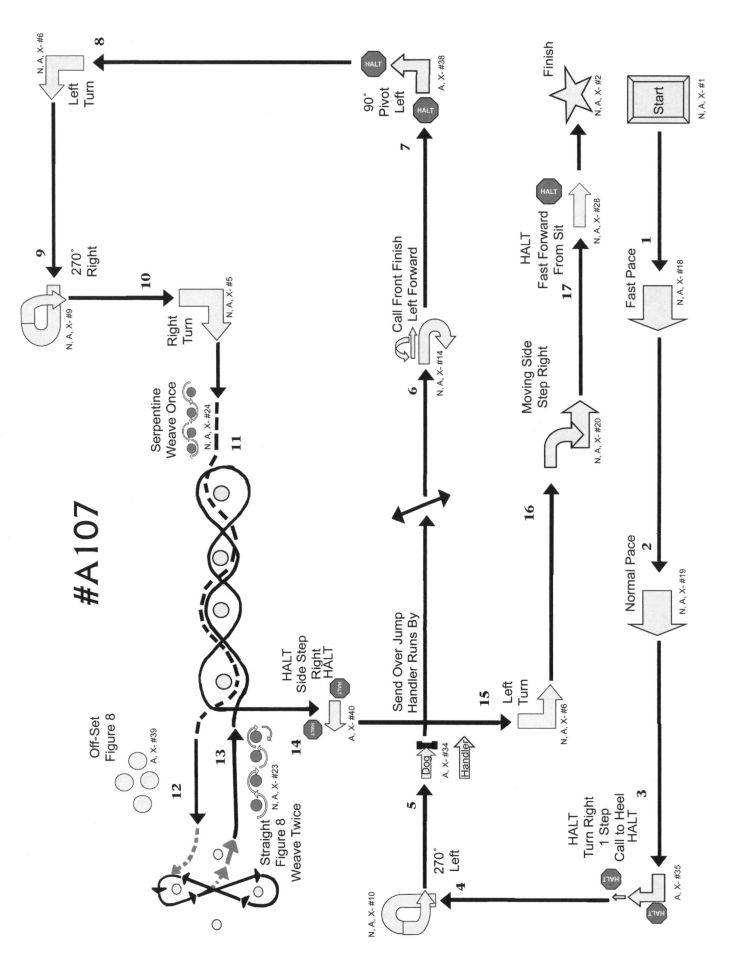

#A107

8 N, A, X- #6 — Left Turn

9 270° Right

10 N, A, X- #9

Right Turn N, A, X- #5

11 Serpentine Weave Once N, A. X- #24

Off-Set Figure 8 A, X- #39

12

13 Straight Figure 8 Weave Twice N, A, X- #23

14 HALT Side Step Right HALT A, X- #40

7 90° Pivot Left A, X- #38 HALT HALT

6 Call Front Finish Left Forward N, A, X- #14

15 Left Turn N, A, X- #6

5 Send Over Jump Handler Runs By Dog A, X- #34 Handler

4 270° Left N, A, X- #10

3 HALT Turn Right 1 Step Call to Heel HALT HALT

16 Moving Side Step Right N, A, X- #20

17 HALT Fast Forward From Sit N, A, X- #28

Finish N, A, X- #2

Start N, A, X- #1

1 Fast Pace N, A, X- #18

2 Normal Pace N, A, X- #19

A, X- #35 HALT

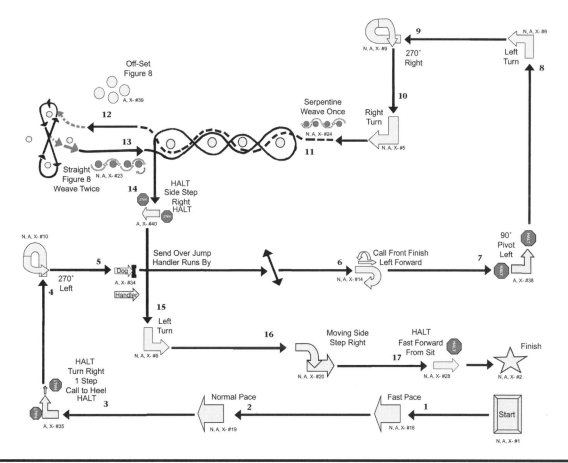

Rally Course #A107

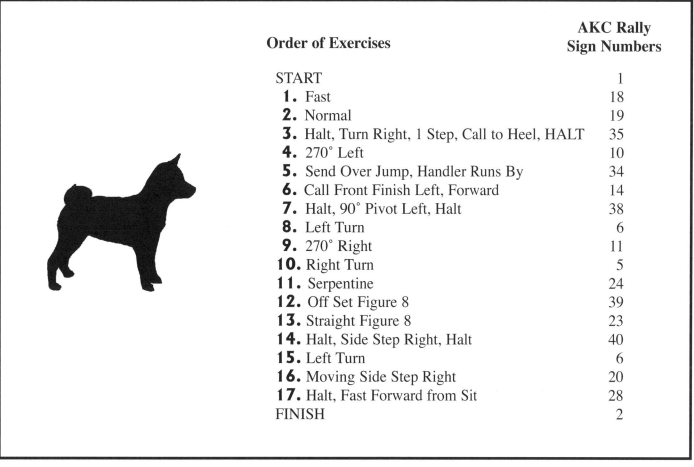

Order of Exercises	AKC Rally Sign Numbers
START	1
1. Fast	18
2. Normal	19
3. Halt, Turn Right, 1 Step, Call to Heel, HALT	35
4. 270° Left	10
5. Send Over Jump, Handler Runs By	34
6. Call Front Finish Left, Forward	14
7. Halt, 90° Pivot Left, Halt	38
8. Left Turn	6
9. 270° Right	11
10. Right Turn	5
11. Serpentine	24
12. Off Set Figure 8	39
13. Straight Figure 8	23
14. Halt, Side Step Right, Halt	40
15. Left Turn	6
16. Moving Side Step Right	20
17. Halt, Fast Forward from Sit	28
FINISH	2

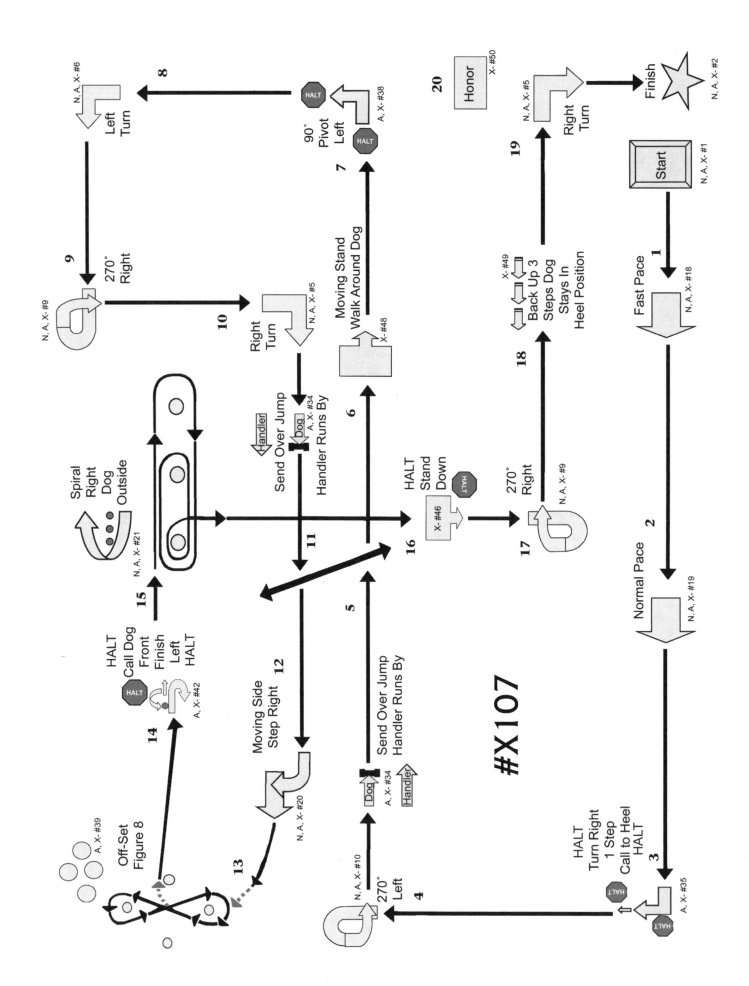

#X107

N, A, X- #6 — **8** — Left Turn

N, A, X- #9 — **9** — 270° Right

10 — Right Turn — N, A, X- #5

HALT — A, X- #38 — **7** — 90° Pivot Left

Moving Stand Walk Around Dog — X- #48

Send Over Jump Handler Runs By — Handler Dog — A, X- #34

6

11

Spiral Right Dog Outside — N, A, X- #21 — **15**

HALT — Call Dog Front Finish Left HALT — A, X- #42 — **14**

Moving Side Step Right — **12** — N, A, X- #20

13

Off-Set Figure 8 — A, X- #39

5 — **16**

Send Over Jump Handler Runs By — Dog Handler — A, X- #34

N, A, X- #10 — **4** — 270° Left

HALT Stand Down — X- #46 — **17** — 270° Right — N, A, X- #9

20 — Honor — X- #50

N, A, X- #5 — **19** — Right Turn — Finish — N, A, X- #2

Start — N, A, X- #1

Fast Pace — **1** — N, A, X- #18

2 — Normal Pace — N, A, X- #19

Back Up 3 Steps Dog Stays In Heel Position — X- #49 — **18**

HALT Turn Right 1 Step Call to Heel HALT — A, X- #35 — **3**

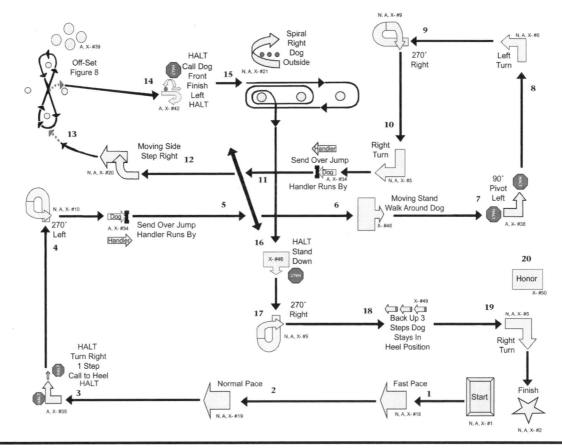

Rally Course #X107

Order of Exercises	AKC Rally Sign Numbers
START	1
1. Fast	18
2. Normal	19
3. Halt, Turn Right 1 Step, Call to Heel, HALT	35
4. 270° Left	10
5. Send Over Jump, Handler Runs By	34
6. Moving Stand, Walk Around Dog	48
7. Halt, 90° Pivot Left, Halt	38
8. Left Turn	6
9. 270° Right	9
10. Right Turn	5
11. Send Over Jump, Handler Runs By	34
12. Moving Side Step Right	20
13. Off Set Figure 8	39
14. Halt, Call Dog Front, Finish Left, Halt	42
15. Spiral Right	21
16. Halt, Stand, Down	46
17. 270° Right	9
18. Back Up 3 Steps, Dog Stays in Heel Position	49
19. Right Turn	5
FINISH	2
20. HONOR	50

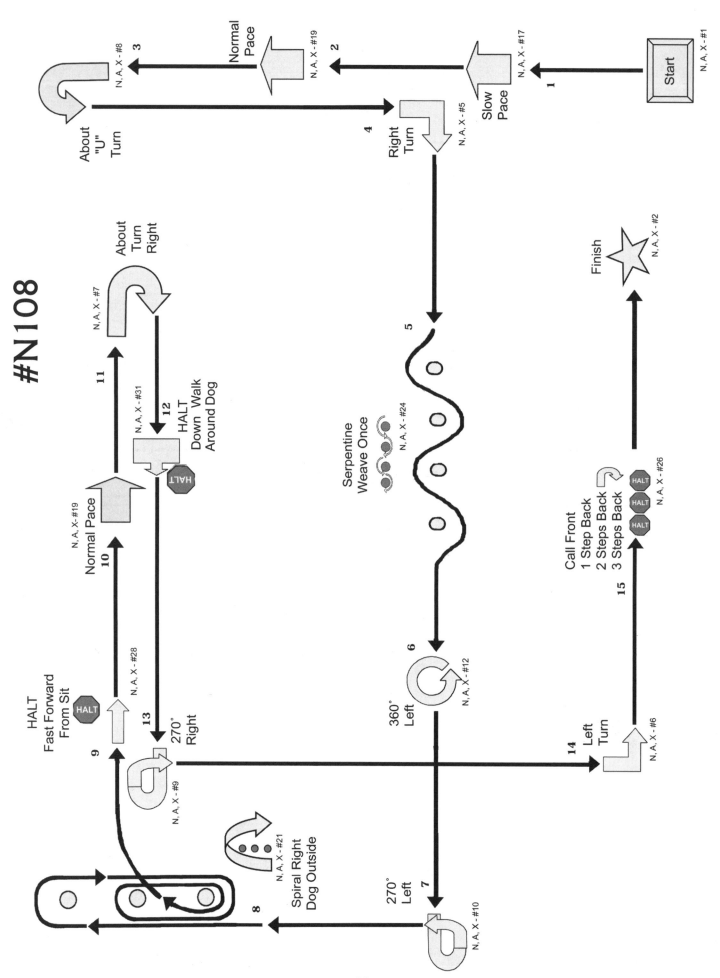

#N108

62

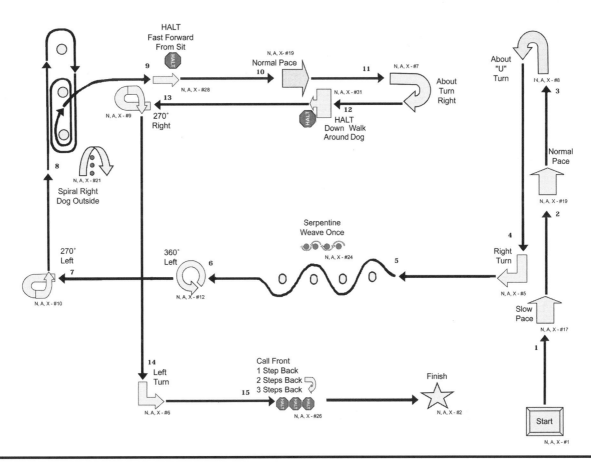

Rally Course #N108

Order of Exercises	AKC Rally Sign Numbers
START	1
1. Slow	17
2. Normal	19
3. About "U" Turn	8
4. Right Turn	5
5. Serpentine	24
6. 360° Left	12
7. 270° Left	10
8. Spiral Right, Dog Outside	21
9. Halt, Fast Forward from Sit	28
10. Normal	19
11. About Turn Right	7
12. Halt, Down, Walk Around Dog	31
13. 270° Right	9
14. Left Turn	6
15. Call Front, 1 Step, 2 Steps, 3 Steps Back	26
FINISH	2

#A108

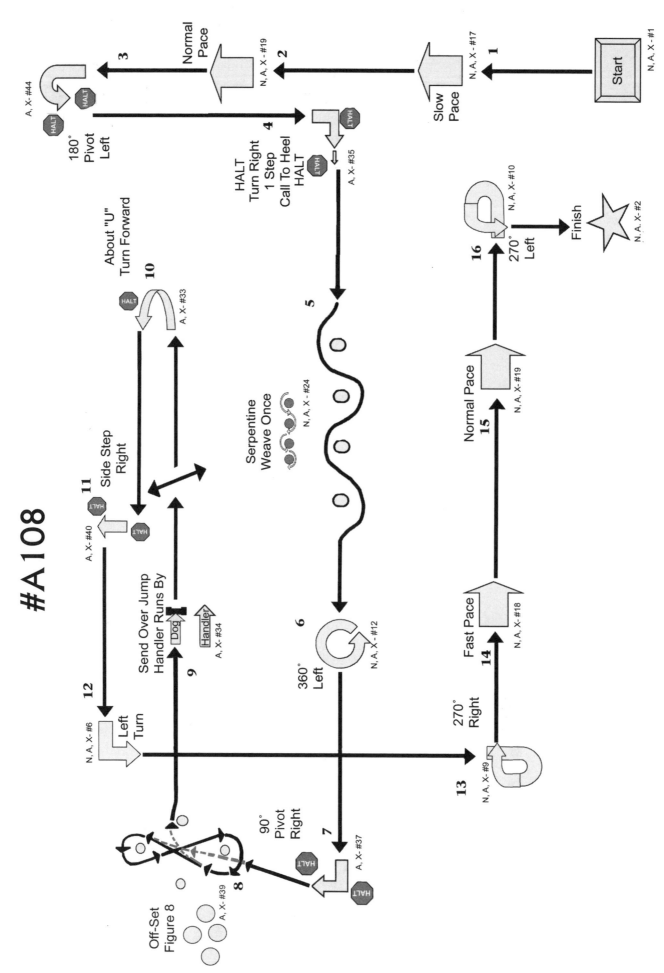

64

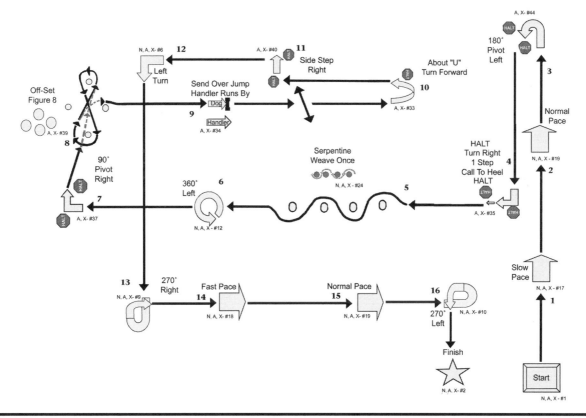

Rally Course #A108

Order of Exercises	AKC Rally Sign Numbers
START	1
1. Slow	17
2. Normal	19
3. Halt, 180° Pivot Left, Halt	44
4. Halt, Turn Right, 1 Step, HALT (call dog to heel)	35
5. Serpentine	24
6. 360° Left	12
7. Halt, 90° Pivot Right, Halt	37
8. Off Set Figure 8	39
9. Send Over Jump, Handler Runs By	34
10. Halt, About "U" Turn	33
11. Halt, Side Step Right, Halt	40
12. Left Turn	6
13. 270° Right	9
14. Fast	18
15. Normal	19
16. 270° Left	10
FINISH	2

#X108

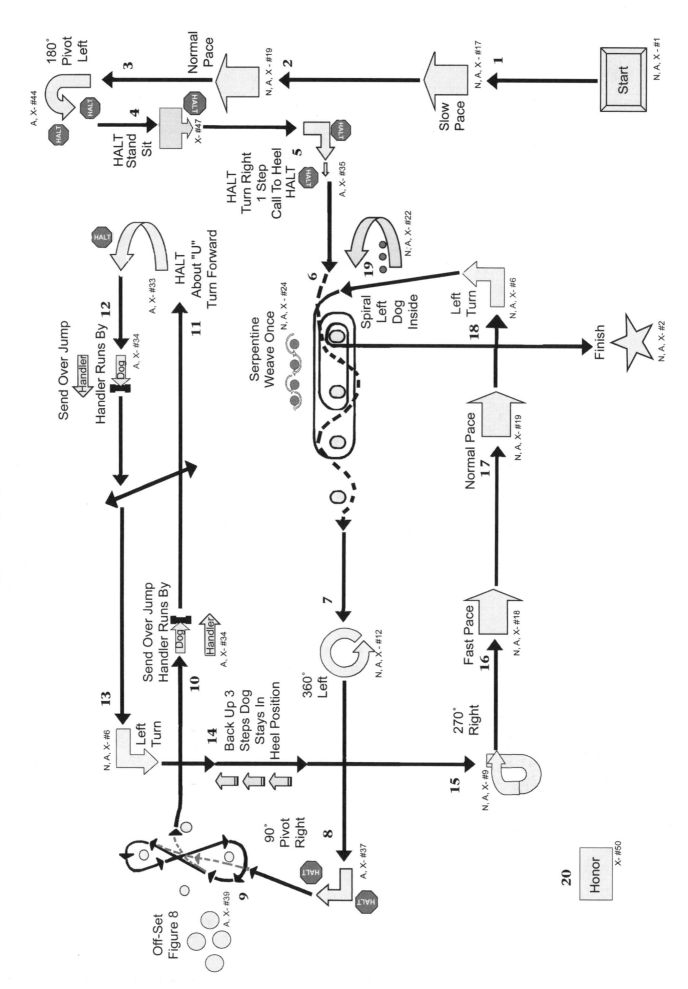

66

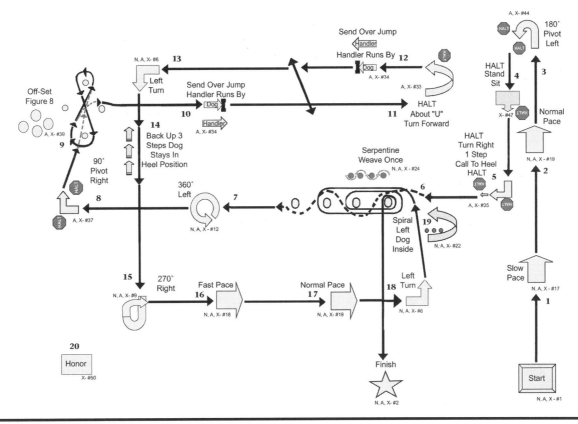

Rally Course #X108

Order of Exercises	AKC Rally Sign Numbers
START	1
1. Slow	17
2. Normal	19
3. Halt, 180° Pivot Left, Halt	44
4. Halt, Stand, Sit	47
5. Halt, Turn Right 1 Step, Halt (call dog to heel)	35
6. Serpentine	24
7. 360° Left	12
8. Halt, 90° Pivot Right, Halt	37
9. Off Set Figure 8	39
10. Send Over Jump, Handler Runs By	34
11. Halt, About "U" Turn, Forward	33
12. Send Over Jump, Handler Runs By	34
13. Left Turn	6
14. Back Up 3, Dog Stays in Heel Position	49
15. 270° Right	9
16. Fast	18
17. Normal	19
18. Left Turn	6
19. Spiral Left, Dog on Inside	22
FINISH	2
20. HONOR	50

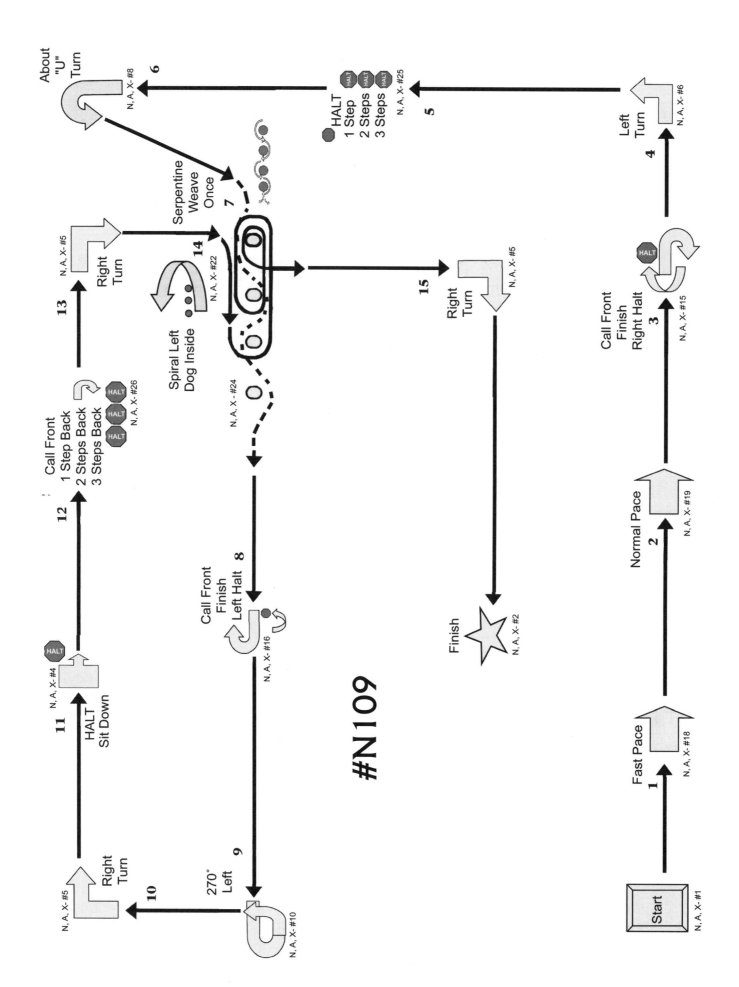

#N109

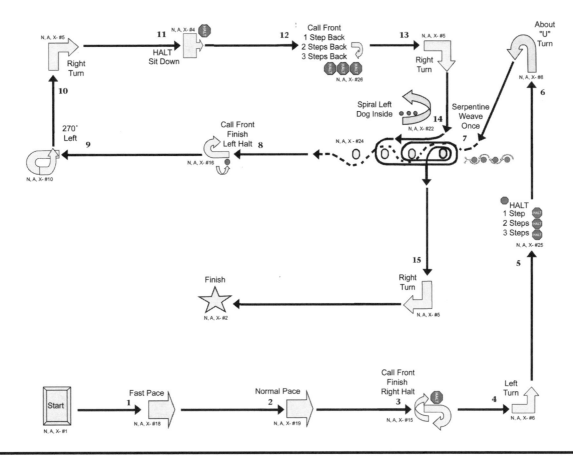

Rally Course #N109

Order of Exercises	AKC Rally Sign Numbers
START	1
1. Fast	18
2. Normal	9
3. Call Front, Finish Right, Halt	15
4. Left Turn	6
5. Halt, 1 Step Halt, 2 Steps Halt, 3 Steps Halt	25
6. About "U" Turn	8
7. Serpentine	24
8. Call Front, Finish Left, Halt	16
9. 270° Left	10
10. Right Turn	5
11. Halt, Down	4
12. Call Front, 1 Step, 2 Steps, 3 Steps Back Halt	26
13. Right Turn	5
14. Spiral Left, Dog Inside	22
15. Right Turn	5
FINISH	2

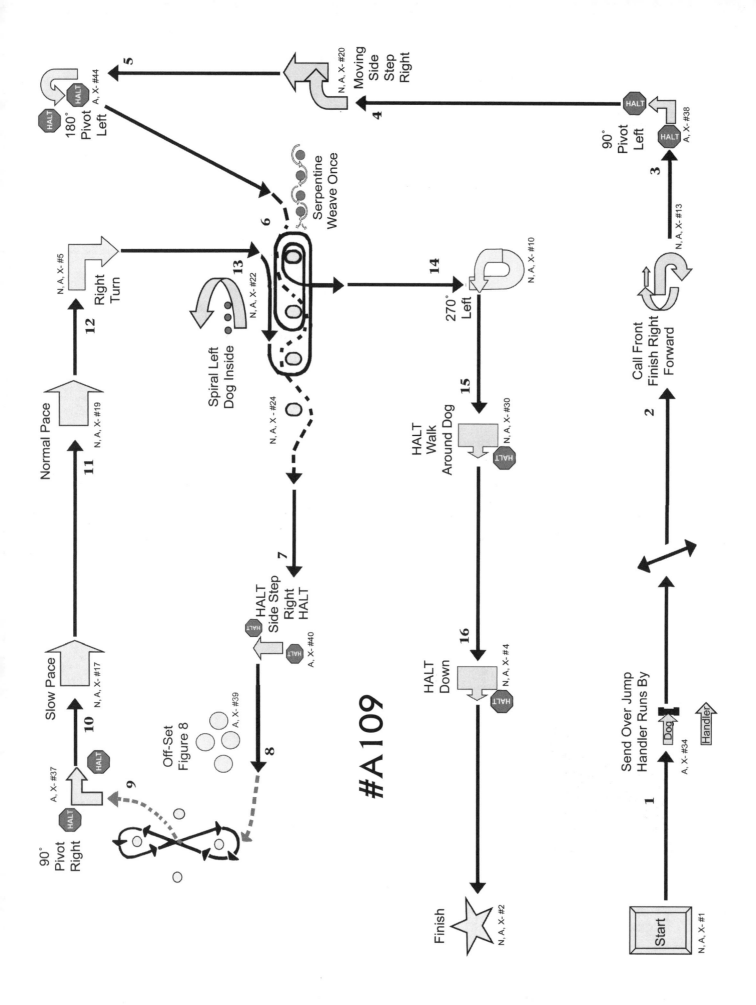

#A109

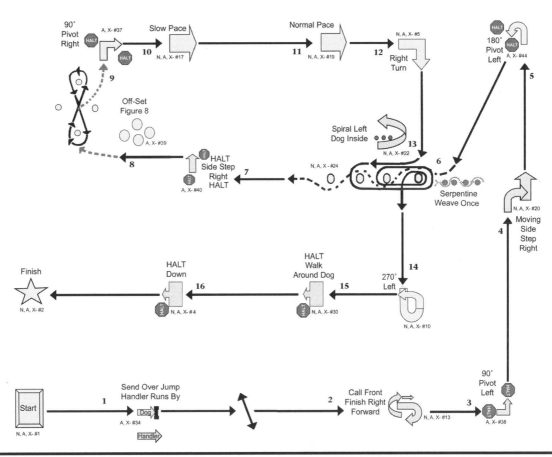

Rally Course #A109

Order of Exercises	AKC Rally Sign Numbers
START	1
1. Send Over Jump, Handler Runs By	34
2. Call Front, Finish Right, Forward	13
3. Halt, 90° Pivot Left, Halt	38
4. Moving Side Step Right	20
5. Halt, 180° Pivot Left, Halt	44
6. Serpentine	24
7. Halt, Side Step Right, Halt	40
8. Off Set Figure 8	39
9. Halt, 90° Pivot Right, Halt	37
10. Slow	17
11. Normal	19
12. Right Turn	5
13. Spiral Left, Dog Inside	22
14. 270° Left	10
15. Halt, Walk Around Dog	30
16. HALT, Down	4
FINISH	2

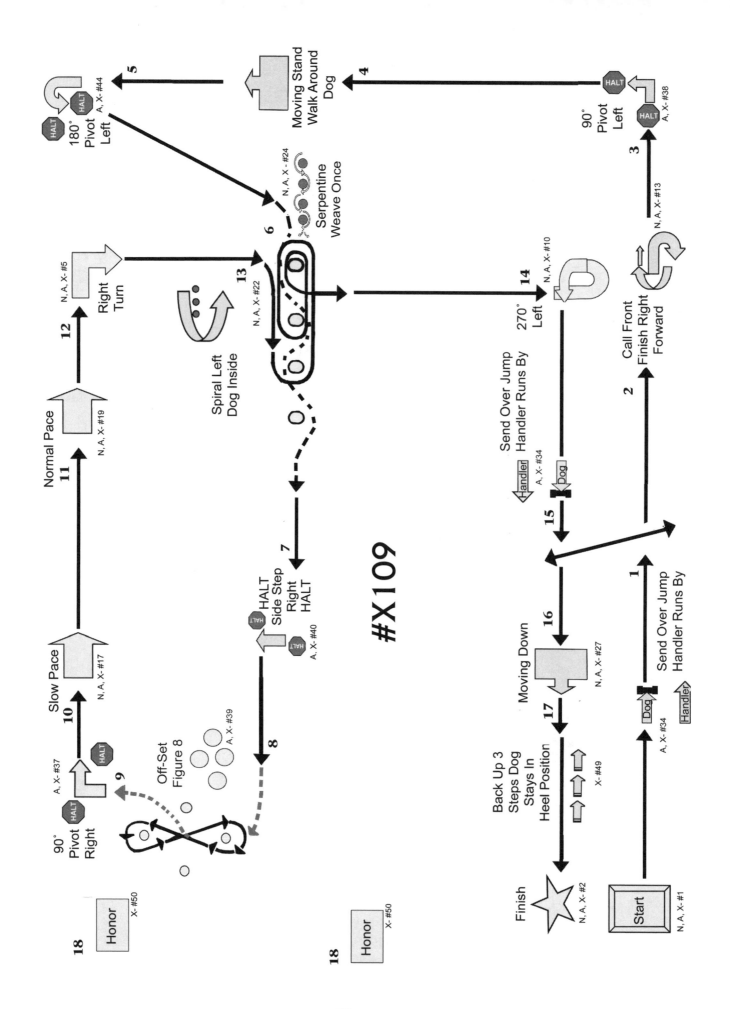

#X109

72

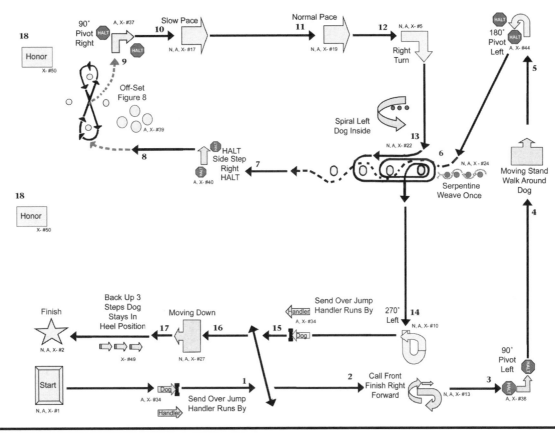

Rally Course #X109

Order of Exercises	AKC Rally Sign Numbers
START	1
1. Send Over Jump, Handler Runs By	34
2. Call Front, Finish Right, Forward	13
3. Halt, 90° Pivot Left, Halt	38
4. Moving Stand, Walk Around Dog	48
5. Halt, 180° Pivot Left, Halt	44
6. Serpentine	24
7. Halt, Side Step Right, Halt	40
8. Off Set Figure 8	39
9. Halt, 90° Pivot Right, Halt	37
10. Slow	17
11. Normal	19
12. Right Turn	5
13. Spiral Left, Dog Inside	22
14. 270° Left	10
15. Send Over Jump, Handler Runs By	34
16. Moving Down	27
17. Back Up 3 Steps, Dog Stays in Heel Position	49
FINISH	2
18. Honor	50

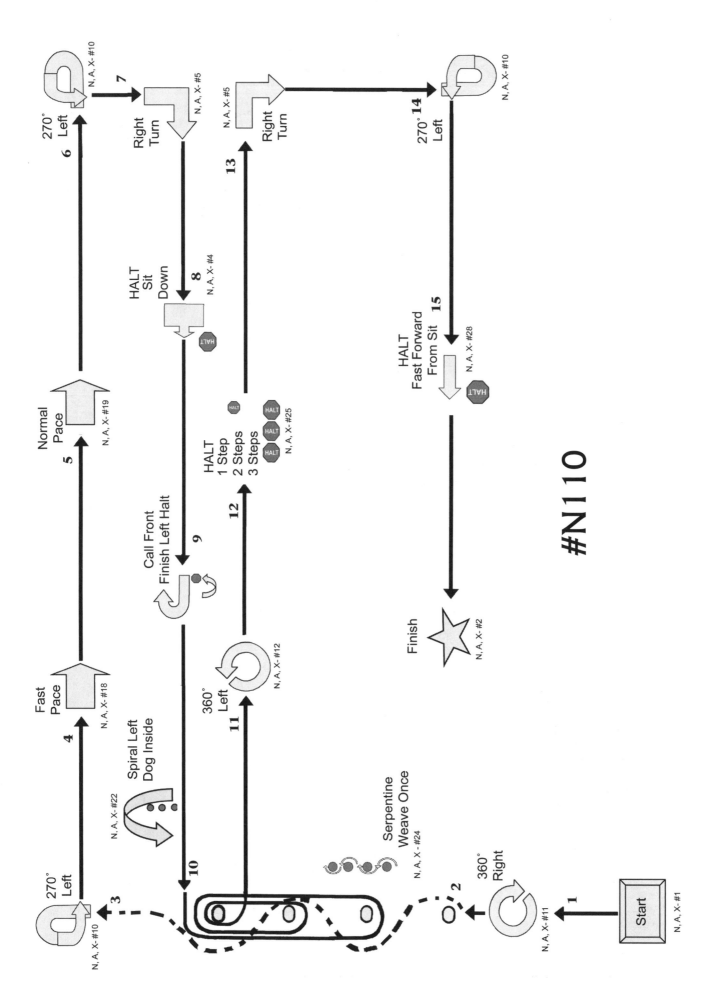

#N110

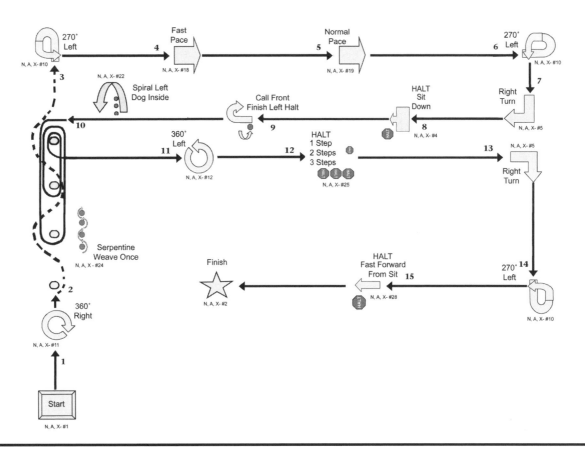

Rally Course #N110

Order of Exercises	AKC Rally Sign Numbers
START	1
1. 360° Right	11
2. Serpentine	24
3. 270° Left	10
4. Fast	18
5. Normal	19
6. 270° Left	10
7. Right Turn	5
8. Halt, Sit, Down	4
9. Call Front, Finish Left, Halt	16
10. Spiral Left, Dog Inside	22
11. 360° Left	12
12. Halt, 1 Step Halt, 2 Steps Halt, 3 Steps Halt	25
13. Right Turn	5
14. 270° Left	10
15. Halt, Fast Forward from Sit	28
FINISH	2

N110

75

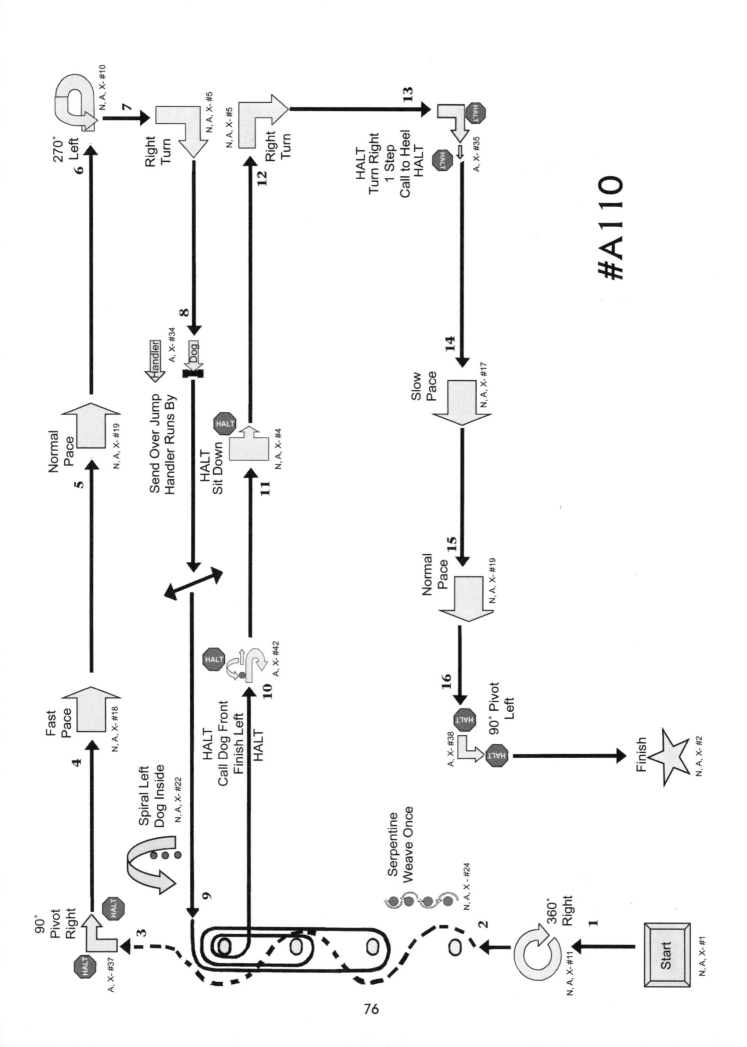

#A110

76

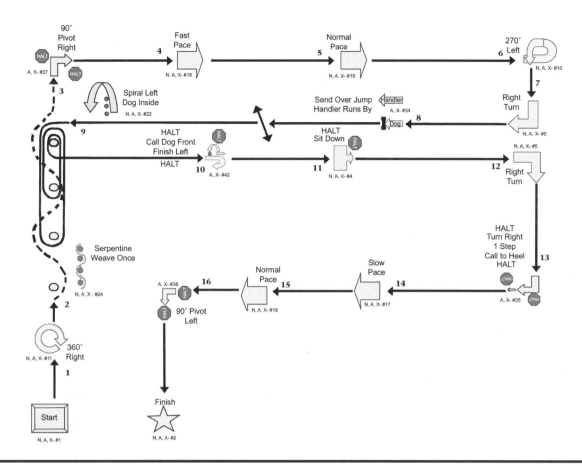

Rally Course #A110

Order of Exercises	AKC Rally Sign Numbers
START	1
1. 360° Right	11
2. Serpentine	24
3. Halt, 90° Pivot Right, Halt	37
4. Fast	18
5. Normal	19
6. 270° Left	10
7. Right Turn	5
8. Send Over Jump, Handler Runs By	34
9. Spiral Left, Dog Inside	22
10. Halt, Call dog Front, Finish Left, Halt	42
11. Halt, Down	4
12. Right Turn	5
13. Halt, Turn Right, 1 Step, Halt, Call to Heel	35
14. Slow	17
15. Normal	1
16. Halt, 90° Pivot Left, Halt	38
FINISH	2

A110

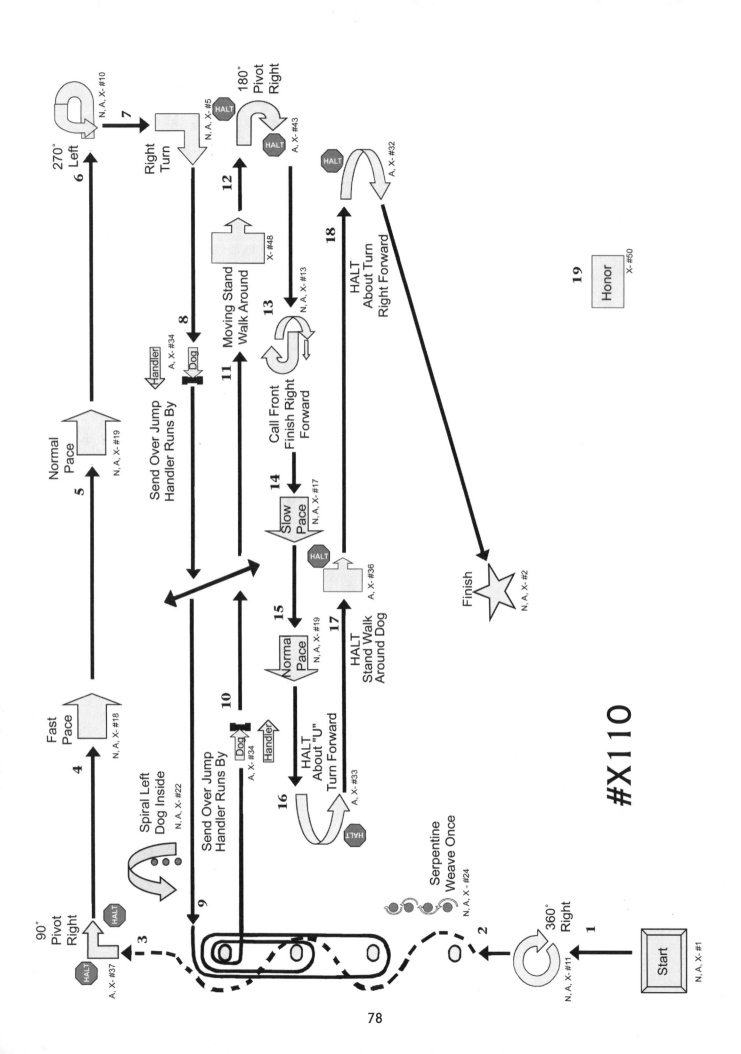

#X110

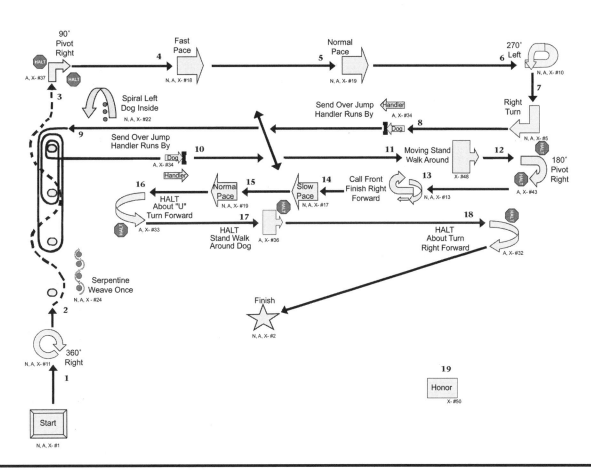

Rally Course #X110

Order of Exercises	AKC Rally Sign Numbers
START	1
1. 360° Right	11
2. Serpentine	24
3. Halt, 90° Pivot Right, Halt	37
4. Fast	18
5. Normal	19
6. 270° Left	10
7. Right Turn	5
8. Send Over Jump, Handler Runs By	34
9. Spiral Left, Dog Inside	22
10. Send Over Jump, Handler Runs By	34
11. Moving Stand, Walk Around Dog	48
12. Halt, 180° Pivot Right, Halt	43
13. Call Front, Finish Left Forward	14
14. Slow	17
15. Normal	19
16. Halt, About "U" Turn Forward	33
17. Halt, Stand, Walk Around Dog	36
18. Halt, About Turn Right Forward	32
FINISH	2
19. Honor	50

X110

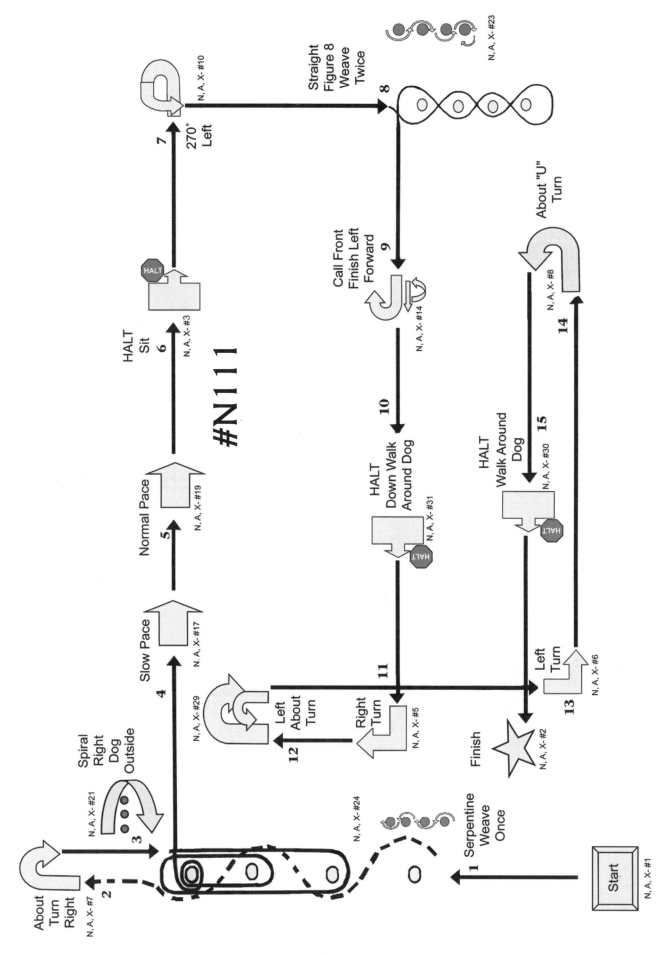

#N111

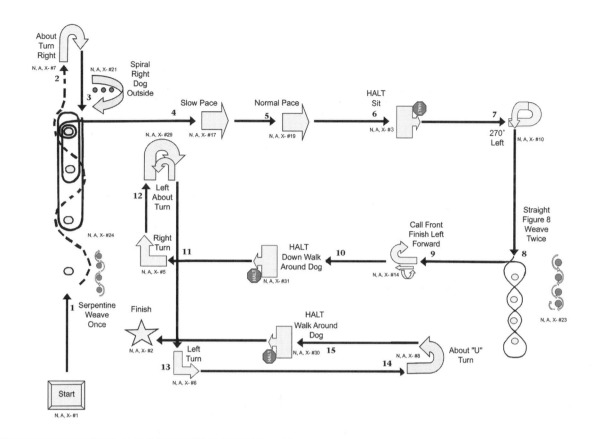

Rally Course #N111

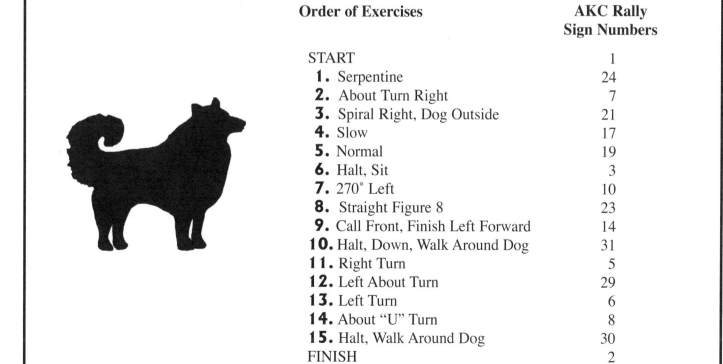

Order of Exercises	AKC Rally Sign Numbers
START	1
1. Serpentine	24
2. About Turn Right	7
3. Spiral Right, Dog Outside	21
4. Slow	17
5. Normal	19
6. Halt, Sit	3
7. 270° Left	10
8. Straight Figure 8	23
9. Call Front, Finish Left Forward	14
10. Halt, Down, Walk Around Dog	31
11. Right Turn	5
12. Left About Turn	29
13. Left Turn	6
14. About "U" Turn	8
15. Halt, Walk Around Dog	30
FINISH	2

#A111

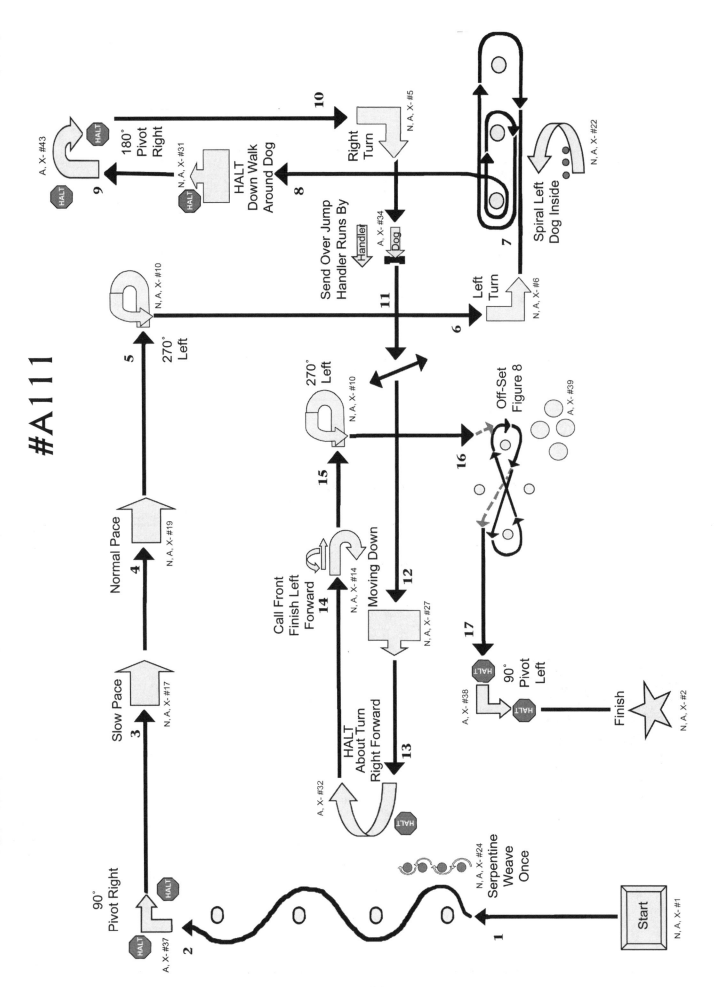

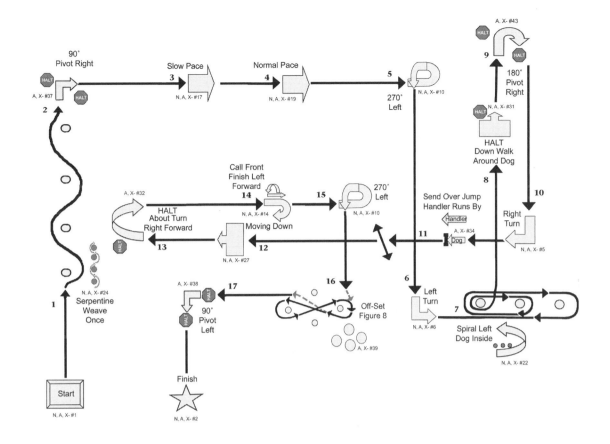

Rally Course #A111

Order of Exercises	AKC Rally Sign Numbers
START	1
1. Serpentine	24
2. Halt, 90° Pivot Right, Halt	37
3. Slow	17
4. Normal	19
5. 270° Left	10
6. Left Turn	6
7. Spiral Left, Dog Inside	22
8. Halt, Down, Walk Around Dog	31
9. Halt, 180° Pivot Right, Halt	43
10. Right Turn	5
11. Send Over Jump, Handler Runs By	34
12. Moving Down	27
13. Halt, About Turn Right Forward	32
14. Call Front, Finish Left, Forward	14
15. 270° Left	10
16. Off Set Figure 8	39
17. Halt, 90° Pivot Left, Halt	38
FINISH	2

A111

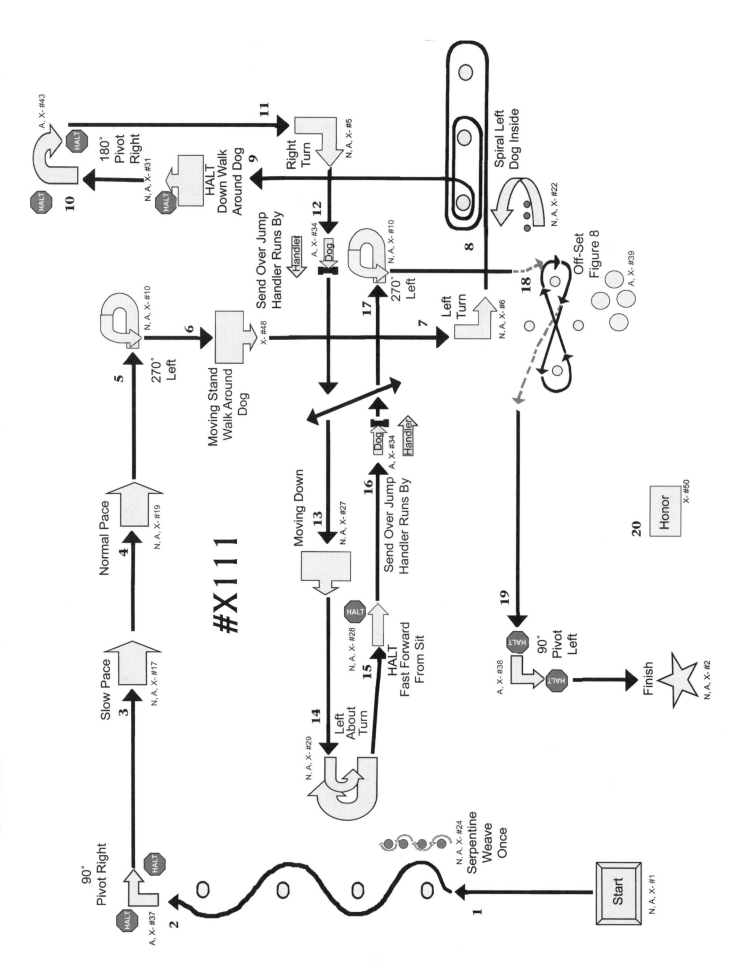

#X111

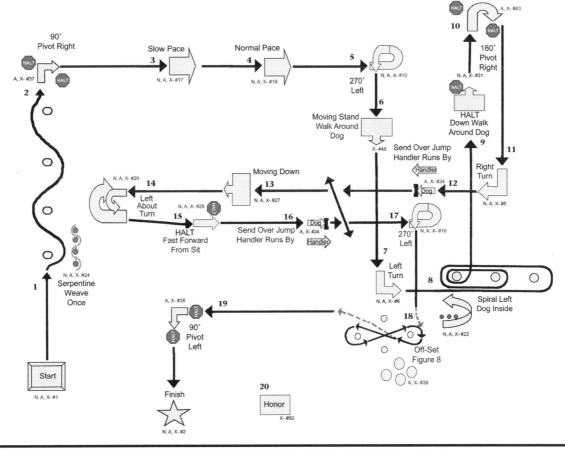

Rally Course #X111

Order of Exercises	AKC Rally Sign Numbers
START	1
1. Serpentine	24
2. Halt, 90° Pivot Right, Halt	37
3. Slow	17
4. Normal	19
5. 270° Left	10
6. Moving Stand, Walk Around Dog	48
7. Left Turn	6
8. Spiral Left, Dog Inside	22
9. Halt, Down, Walk Around Dog	31
10. Halt, 180° Pivot Right, Halt	43
11. Right Turn	5
12. Send Over Jump, Handler Runs By	34
13. Moving Down	27
14. Left About Turn	29
15. Halt, Fast Forward from Sit	28
16. Send Over Jump, Handler Runs By	34
17. 270° Left	10
18. Off Set Figure 8	39
19. Halt, 90° Pivot Left, Halt	38
FINISH	2
20. Honor	50

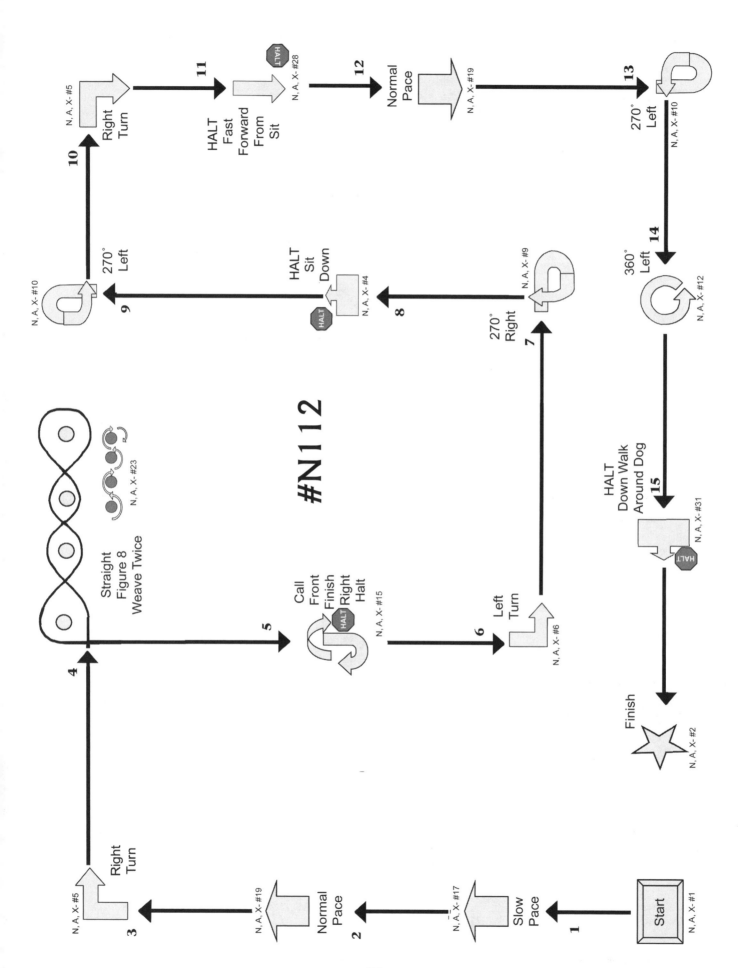

#N112

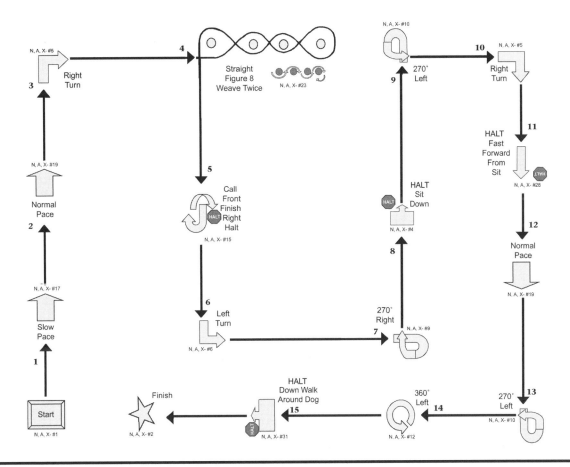

Rally Course #N112 (40x50 short course)

Order of Exercises	AKC Rally Sign Numbers
START	1
1. Slow	17
2. Normal	19
3. Right Turn	5
4. Straight Figure 8	23
5. Call Front, Finish Right, Halt	15
6. Left Turn	6
7. 270° Right	9
8. Halt, Down	4
9. 270° Left	10
10. Right Turn	5
11. Halt, Fast Forward from Sit	28
12. Normal	19
13. 270° Left	10
14. 360° Left	12
15. Halt, Down, Walk Around Dog	31
FINISH	2

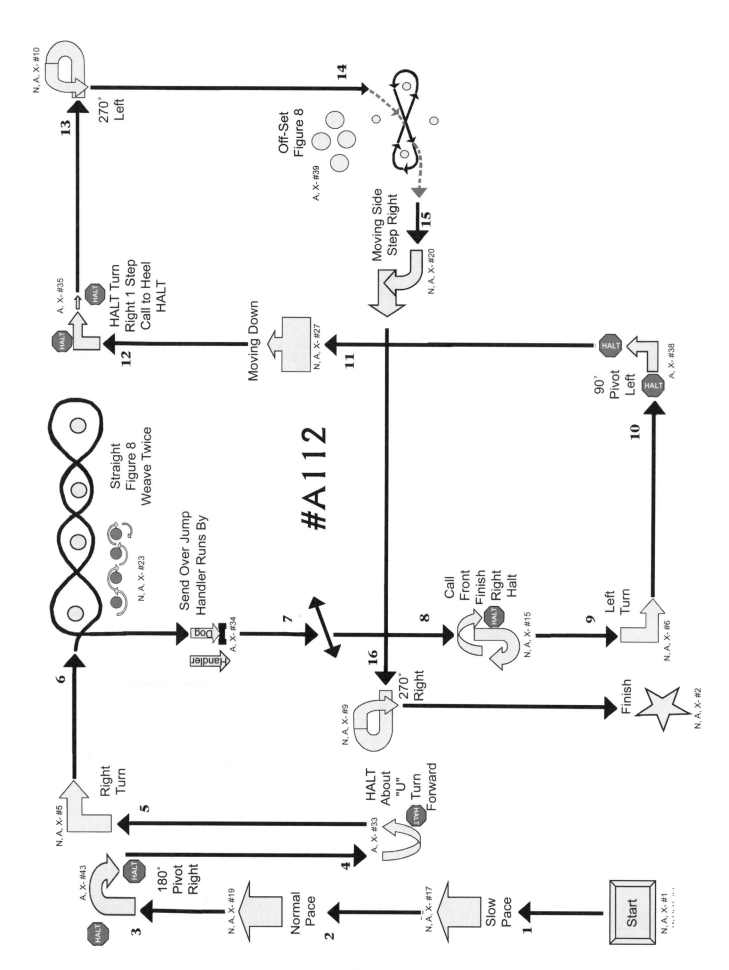

#A112

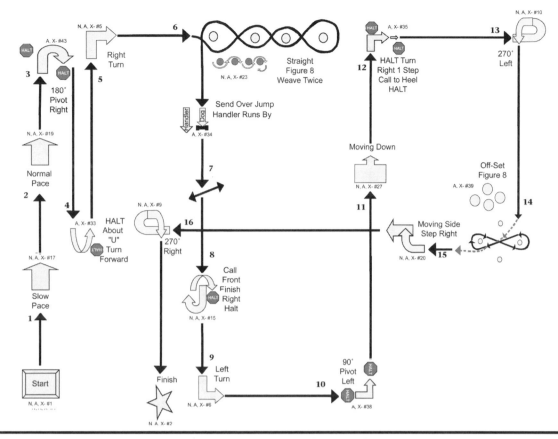

Rally Course #A112 (40x50 short course)

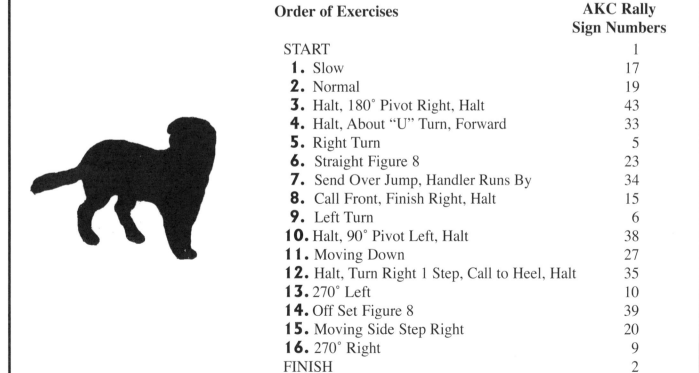

Order of Exercises	AKC Rally Sign Numbers
START	1
1. Slow	17
2. Normal	19
3. Halt, 180° Pivot Right, Halt	43
4. Halt, About "U" Turn, Forward	33
5. Right Turn	5
6. Straight Figure 8	23
7. Send Over Jump, Handler Runs By	34
8. Call Front, Finish Right, Halt	15
9. Left Turn	6
10. Halt, 90° Pivot Left, Halt	38
11. Moving Down	27
12. Halt, Turn Right 1 Step, Call to Heel, Halt	35
13. 270° Left	10
14. Off Set Figure 8	39
15. Moving Side Step Right	20
16. 270° Right	9
FINISH	2

A112

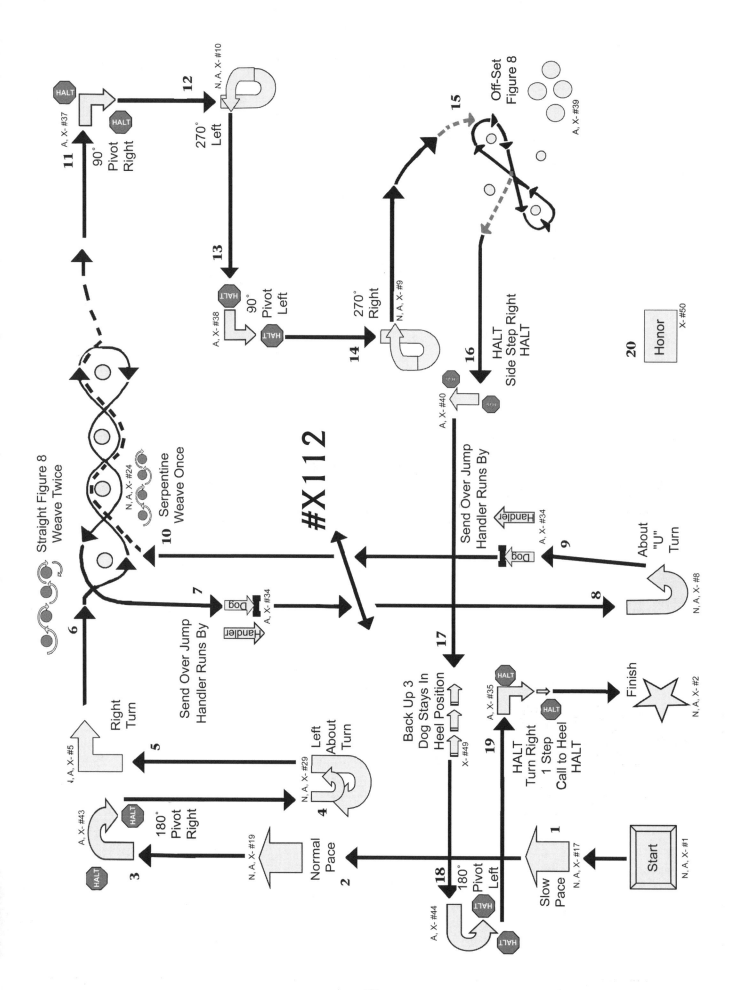

#X112

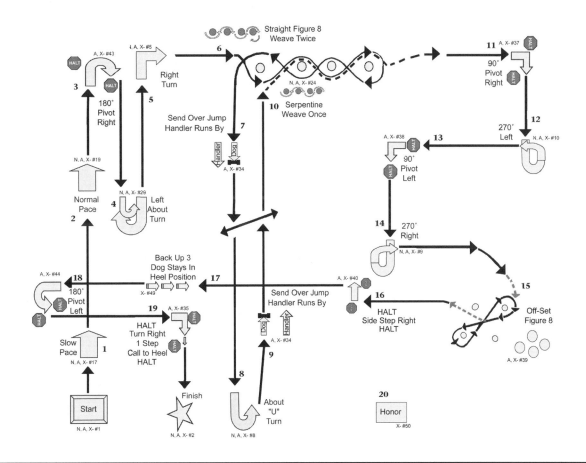

Rally Course #X112 (40x50 short course)

Order of Exercises	AKC Rally Sign Numbers
START	1
1. Slow	17
2. Normal	19
3. Halt, 180° Pivot Right, Halt	43
4. Left About Turn	29
5. Right Turn	5
6. Straight Figure 8	23
7. Send Over Jump, Handler Runs By	34
8. About "U" Turn Forward	8
9. Send Over Jump, Handler Runs By	34
10. Serpentine	24
11. Halt, 90° Pivot Right	37
12. 270° Left	10
13. Halt, 90° Pivot Left	38
14. 270° Right	9
15. Off Set Figure 8	39
16. Halt, Side Step Right, Halt	40
17. Back Up 3 Steps, Dog Stays in Heel	49
18. Halt, 180° Pivot Left, Halt	44
19. Halt, Turn Right 1 Step, Halt	35
FINISH	2
20. HONOR	50

X112